CW00919990

King Twist

King Twist

A portrait of Frank Randle

Jeff Nuttall

Routledge & Kegan Paul
London, Henley and Boston

First published in 1978
by Routledge & Kegan Paul Ltd
39 Store Street,
London WC1E 7DD,
Broadway House,
Newtown Road,
Henley-on-Thames,
Oxon RG9 1EN and
9 Park Street,
Boston, Mass. 02108, USA
Photoset in 11 on 12 Baskerville by
Kelly and Wright, Bradford-on-Avon, Wiltshire
and printed in Great Britain by
Lowe & Brydone Printers Ltd, Thetford, Norfolk
Plates printed by
Headley Bros. Ltd, Ashford, Kent

British Library Cataloguing in Publication Data

Nuttall, Jeff
King Twist.
1. Randle, Frank   2. Comedians — England —
Biography
I. Title
791   092   4   PN2598.R/   78-40548

ISBN 0 7100 8977 5

Contents

Illustrations

Author's note

In writing a book about a man who is long dead one is limited in one's sources to hearsay, myth, journalism, rumour and memory, none of which is notable for reliable verity.

This portrait, then, makes unashamed use of the aura of tales and ideas surrounding the memory of a man whose charisma was powerful in his own lifetime and who has complicated the issue by romancing freely about his own past wherever he went. Where accounts are in direct contradiction both versions have been included. In any case my document makes no pretence to objective truth, leaving the reader to assess the quality of the material rather than note anything as though it were ascertained fact. Thus I hope to have achieved a deeper truth about the climate of a time that is almost gone.

I am, of course, deeply indebted to all those people who have ransacked their memories and the backs of their bureau drawers in order to help me make this book as varied and exciting as its subject. All of them are mentioned in detail in the narrative, but special gratitude is extended to the *Blackpool Gazette and Herald* for their painstaking assistance, to George Barnes, and also to Messrs Palmer and Turner, for their informative book *The Blackpool Story*.

Jeff Nuttall

Overture: concrete

I am looking for a memory to defend me. I am exposed and threatened. I need a myth and I need a hero.

The rolling eye of a manic little lecher scorches through the years. I recall a billygoat toper, a varicosed buttock-pincher, a dyspeptic ale-swiller. I need him and I'm setting out to find him.

The Joseph brothers run the City Varieties, Leeds. To see them I must go through a town they still call Bradford. I shall not go by tram and steam train. I shall go by Diesel bus and Diesel train. The place they still call Bradford will not be a smoky bustling warren of snickets, cobbled alleyways, rag shops, warehouses and crammed boozers. It will be in no way different from any other city on the island. Glass and concrete. Nationwide chain stores. Adman's consumer goods. Cheap chic and pedestrian precincts with rockeries made of real granite that somehow, in this setting, look as though they were papier mâché.

I shall not go through a place that rubs off on me as it once did, both psychologically and literally. I shall pass with ease and speed and absolutely no identity through a place like any other place that doesn't know me and doesn't want to.

I am going to see the Joseph brothers in Leeds because they might help me to find a hero who, in turn, might in some way

defend me against a tide that is rising over my country steeply
and rapidly. It can't be called a tide of whizz-kid executives
drifting elegantly in and out of the unbelievably tedious,
muted and carpeted areas of the Norfolk Gardens Hotel. The
Norfolk Gardens is Bradford's rectangular slab of commuter
luxury in the current cut-price Hilton manner. It can't really
be called a tide of visiting Krauts who get off the plane at
Yeadon, go to the Norfolk Gardens or the Leeds Dragonara,
watch telly, attend their board meeting, eat their meal, drink
their drinks, watch telly and then depart. The tide isn't
human. It is grey. It is concrete. The motorway is concrete and
there is only one. The city centre is concrete and there is only
one. A legion of spotty boffins who see themselves as civic
thinkers are paving my country over because they think that
this is the way the window must be dressed for those smartly
shod angels who bear the economic miracle over the sea. A
legion of men no one has ever seen is disguising my country as
Dusseldorf. I am journeying anonymous through the rising
tide of concrete in search of a man, a memory, that will act as
a talisman against an age that is somehow trying to cancel me
out.

The search will take me into corners and havens into which
the concrete hasn't yet penetrated. I must find similar souls
who, like me, are threatened or who, unlike me, are so deep in
the trappings of an old warm culture that they haven't noticed
the danger.

Eric Gill put me on to the Josephs. I met him in Whitelock's,
Leeds. To get to Whitelock's you pass through the pedestrian
precinct. The uniform city centre always has one. You pass
through the Leeds one. Behind the concrete you can see the
brick, sandblasted now but none the less brick, and in some
places you can see holes in the façade, doorways that escaped
the designer, alleys not yet sealed. To get to Whitelock's you
enter one of these and suddenly you're free. You've escaped the
buggers. The rotting bricks, the crazy flagstones, the cobbles,
the exposed plumbing, slabs of flaking plaster, have been
waiting all along, like some loved and geriatric parent you'd
thought dead. Maybe Frank Randle himself will prove in some
way to be still alive, waiting patiently in the fundamental
human areas from which his humour sprang, gurgling,

gargling, belching and leaking while the world tidies up its image and streamlines its behaviour.

Whitelock's is a haven for a different kind of executive from those who are checking in down at the Dragonara. An affectionately preserved Edwardian restaurant bar with the art-nouveau glass and brasswork of the traditional oyster bar, it harbours the fraternity of the jaunty waistcoat and the blunt word. The office workers, junior representatives and the old warhorses of nineteenth-century trade in so far as it survives in Leeds. Its drama is invigorated by the earthy juxtaposition of money and regional accent. It is not working class and it is not exclusive. It is a pub where you meet those members of the business world who relish the flavour of the town in which they operate, who would never wish to escape to Dusseldorf or Boston.

Eric Gill is a printing-union representative. His face is a mass of wry smirks, twinkling guffaws, amazed concern, concerned amazement. Gilly is a pub man and wears all the mobile masks of a man who lives amongst crowds.

'Frank Randle?' he says. 'My God! You might try the Joseph brothers at the City Varieties. Michael Joseph particularly.'

More pints of Younger's mild. 'Michael Joseph, yes. Tell him I sent you.'

And another such hole in the concrete façade of the city centre is the shallow alley that forms the entrance to the City Varieties. A playbill advertising Nat Jackley in the forth-coming panto. Photographs. Lights.

'Mr Joseph? In the office round the back. Outside, turn right, right 'gain, then right again.'

Again, old Leeds. The cobbles, the irregular off-verticals of the houses. Gutter litter, a coming and going of the people that make things tick. Delivery boys, vanmen, messengers, cleaners, street sweepers.

The office is busy. Mr Joseph will be available in fifteen minutes. A spacious pub, then, like Whitelock's, not re-created or imitated but preserved. Aspidistra and dark carpet. Red plush seats. A barmaid with a voice like a circular saw. Two doubles and back to see the Josephs.

Michael Joseph is small, collected, friendly, businesslike and always short of time. He is a member of that select company of abstemious Jews who administrate legions of performers dedicated to the immoderate. All his life he has moved amongst characters so extravagant that, as the concrete rises, they beggar belief. When the concrete façade is complete, when you and I and everybody else has been paved over, no one will believe that there were such people. Mr Joseph has moved among them with the tact and quiet patience of a nurse, taking his 10 per cent and remembering that what everyone else thinks is madness, fantasy, carnival is, in fact, business.

'Randle? Well . . . not sure I can help you. . . . Try the British Music Hall Society perhaps. Maybe my brother. . . .' Is he suspicious of me? I am tartly aware that I am not, myself, in the business.

Stanley Joseph is bigger, different, not so dapper or self-contained as his brother, is far more extrovert. 'Randle? Oh yes. Well, right on top you know. Top money, a star. . . . Temperament? Well, we never saw any. Always reliable. There on time. Sober on stage.' Why should he make such a point of this?

'Tough man, you know. Powerful. Had been a boxer, I believe. Strong personality. One of the greatest. Absolute tops. A very very funny man.'

So in the first tentative leg of my search I've drawn a bit of a blank. I've got a whiff of a professional loyalty that will give away no secrets, peddle no scandal. There is something that is being kept from me. If it is worth hiding it must be worth looking for.

I've touched the fuss and fret of a business everybody thought was dead and I've got a breath of a world where the pit orchestra's tinsel sound drifts jauntily through to the bar. A world where gin is the drink and the demeanour buoyant, undefeated. I will have my myth. The music is not far distant and promises well.

PART I

A Jewel on the Nation's Arse

1

The nation organises its functioning into its separate areas.

London and the South East form the head. Here are the offices and the council chambers, the counting houses and the libraries, the two great universities, the face to be presented to strangers.

The dancing extremities are the Celtic hinterlands. Here is the folklore and the idiosyncrasy and the poetry.

The throbbing, loamish heart is rural. The West Country, East Anglia, North Yorkshire. Here are the finest cathedrals, the wheat, the livestock, the best soil.

And the tripes, the guts, the root body functions are in the Industrial North. It is an endearing characteristic of the nation in its nineteenth-century structure that it is frank with its functioning. Like the hidden back alleys of Leeds, it lets its plumbing show. The difference between the rash of railways, cheap terrace housing, arrogant chimneys, mills and sweat-shops, stations and wreckage yards, warehouses and sewerage beds that covers most of Lancashire and half Yorkshire, the difference between that rash and the encroaching layer of concrete, is that one is a boastful disporting of the nation's crude workshops and the other is a bureaucratic cosmetic, the uncluttered face presented by a business world in which the board of directors never sees the factory and the money is shuttled into a Swiss vault by computer.

This rash, then, this ostentatious defilement of the landscape, is the cradle of English politics, where the boss was a face not a trade mark and the extent of his wealth could be gauged by the length of his excretory chimney.

The nation's digestive system and anal tract is coiled across the Pennines and dredges down across the desolate plain of West Lancashire to the Irish Sea. Here, stretched between Preston and Morecambe, is the Fylde, a flat coastland of rank marshes, of meandering potholed lanes, hedgeless sedges and damp private gardens enclosing secretive houses that look as though the dead inhabitant, posed by Hitchcock, may lie crumbling before a stuttering television and a smoking grate in the front parlour. Here, where the sea is brown with the effluvia of the whole conurbation, lies Blackpool, the jewel of the North, a gaudy gem set on the nation's arse.

Two hundred years ago Blackpool was a row of pubs and bowling greens along the coast road, a small tenth-rate imitation of an élite spa-retreat with attendant tradesmen. It was a symptomatic part of the general lot of the Lancashire mill worker, that pale, hardy character whom Cobden and Bright insisted was the historic peer of the peasant, that virtuoso of the desolate wit and the clog dance, symptomatic that such a featureless stretch of coastland should be his nearest access to the sea.

One can imagine the early horse-drawn wagonettes setting out from Salford in bleak dawns, wandering with their hampers of tripe and bottled beer, cold sweet tea and potato sandwiches, wending towards those vast sands where the sewerage of the growing cotton towns swung in great green breakers against the jetty. One can see the faces, pale and anaemic with wide hurt eyes, with swaggart twinkling eyes, with eyes of defiant puritanism, faces so pale they are nearly green. The delicate pink areas around nostrils and mouth-corners. Prototype faces for the comedians' coat of Number Five and a lining of Lake. Faces under stocking hats and bonnets, faces in a row looking out on that grey sea. One can hear the impenetrable humour, sceptical, unimpressed, tough, pessimistic: 'There were no wrecks and nobody drownded. In fact, nowt t' laugh at at all.'

They had come, however, to be impressed. They had come to ogle. Women of quality were being born fully draped from the horse-drawn bathing machines and immersed in those cloudy breakers. Postures were being struck along the cliff walks by men of substance. Tumblers of sea water were to be had in the inns and, whilst the magical health was to be enjoyed that had previously been the privilege of the leisured class, modes of behaviour were also to be imbibed. At that early stage the advertised commodity was health but the real commodity was style. Style was to be seen on the bowling greens, in the saloon bar of the Victoria Hotel, in the hundred-yard promenade room of Dr Cocker's Victoria Assembly Rooms, in the Assembly Rooms' shops and billiard parlour, along the queues for the Liverpool-Barrow steamship, or from Dr Cocker himself as he displayed himself along the sleepy streets in the only wheeled vehicle in the borough. They had come to ogle and they had come to learn, and, even though some would have to share their seat by alternate stints of walking all the way back to Salford on a bellyful of ale, brine and ozone, they would be back. Back to operate the same alternate shift system with beds in Henry Banks's sea-front boarding-house, eventually back by rail up the branch line from Poulton le Fylde. Chapel and church, later the Lancashire and Yorkshire Railway itself, would fix them up with excursion trains composed of any rolling stock to hand. Those pale, grimy faces would cram cattle trucks. Those skinny flanks would balance on precarious splintery planks. 'SEA BATHING FOR THE WORKING CLASSES' said the posters, three bob from Manchester, two and a kick from Bolton, two bob from Chorley and Preston. Leave Manchester Victoria at 6 a.m. Climb down on the far side of the peat marsh at 9. Start back at 6 p.m. Home by 9. 'Parties availing themselves of these trains will be enabled to BATHE AND REFRESH THEMSELVES in ample time to attend a Place of Worship.'

On 1 July 1849 two engines would pull fifty-five carriages from Rochdale to join another train of the same length from Stalybridge. Two trains from Manchester with twenty-five and thirty-six carriages respectively would join the convoy and finally twenty-eight more carriages from Bolton. This vast cavalcade would discharge some 10,000 cotton workers and colliers into this straggling mile of boozers and boarding-houses where there was still no street lighting and no tap water. Rickety legs would waddle down Talbot Street, through Talbot Square, past the Clifton Arms, to the point where the rubble from the railway excavations formed the blunt promontory from which the North Pier would eventually grow. Over the cliffs their clogs would take them to where three wooden negroes surmounted Uncle Tom's Cabin. There they could buy tea and comemmorate the occasion with an American Portrait, and there, with the dogged energy of working people, they would dance till home time.

Blackpool's pretence to gentility, always somewhat tenuous through the desolate setting and the absence of any real spa, was eroded further by its proximity to the Manchester cotton towns, yet further by the appetite of the new urban working class to get it as good as the gaffers, and ultimately by the opportunism first of the Talbot-Clifton family, locals Henry Banks and his son-in-law Dr Cocker, Messrs Parks and Taylor, and finally through the participation of retired industrialists, particularly from Halifax, who, having grown fat enough to retire on the backs of the poor, now proceeded to embellish their latter years with their late employees' annual savings. 'SEA BATHING FOR THE WORKING CLASSES' set the tone for a rocketing local industry whose stock in trade was the best, for the poor, cheap. The water being laid on, the promenade built and lit, North and Central Piers constructed to launch the day-trippers to Douglas, the Talbot Square Assembly Rooms (complete with Free Library and Theatre Royal built in) open and thriving, having built the Winter Gardens as a monument to retained gentility, the first electric street light in Britain having exploded in the smoke-clouded minds of the visitors all along the front, Blackpool decided somewhere around 1879 to begin to play down the gentility bit. In the same year as electric light hit Britain, all along the Fylde coast, a man from the back of the audience (one of the most distinguished anonymous Englishmen) interrupted Miss Ellen Lamb's song recital with, 'Give us a comic song!' The *Blackpool Herald* declared: 'Blackpool is becoming a place where the people expect to have a jolly care-for-nothing sort of scamper rather than avail themselves of the benefit of the sea breezes — During the best months of the year the town is deluged by the lower classes and it would be unreasonable to expect the higher grades of society to mix with them.' This was the year when the Winter Gardens' manager, Bill Holland, having been warned that the hundred-guinea carpet he had laid in his Grand Pavilion would be spat upon by working-class trippers, printed posters inviting the world to 'come and spit on Bill Holland's hundred guinea carpet'.

The cotton famine following the American Civil War delayed things somewhat. The financial crises of the late seventies didn't help at the time. However, when retail prices were lowered in the early eighties, and wages stayed level, it became obvious to Cocker, Sergenson who ran the Theatre Royal on little more than a thin diet of East Lynn, Holland who had come from London music hall with a banner of vulgarity on which was emblazoned the motto: 'Give 'Em What They Want', and Mayor Bickerstaff who had ideas about Cocker's Aquarium and Menagery, that 't' brass were forthcoming' from the day-tripping mill workers rather than the concert-going hotel guests. Watering-place gentility was tactfully banished to the cliff walks between Uncle Tom's Cabin and Talbot Square. Sarah Bernhardt, summoned to perform her blood-coughing triumph as 'La Dame Aux Camelias', was inaudible in the acoustically disastrous Winter Gardens Pavilion and was, in any case, speaking French to an audience many of whom couldn't even read English. 'Speak up, lass,' cried the Voice at the Back. 'Nobbut a soul can 'ear what th'art sayin'. We 'aven't paid fort' like o' that.' The divine Sarah fled in mid-performance (money was returned, profitably to those adroit enough to move into the expensive rows) and wrote indignantly to the management, 'Je suis une artiste et non une exhibition.' Sergenson, who was about to build the Grande Theatre for a policy of popular material, ran the statement off as a poster to ridicule his rival. One Mr Walton, resident comedian at the Prince of Wales, knocked 'em out with the entrance line, 'Je suis une exhibition et non une artiste.'

The scene was set and the big entrepreneurs moved in. Holland, 'the people's caterer', built the Opera House into the Winter Gardens complex to make it the home of lavish spectacle where John Tiller, founder of the clockwork follies, directed 'Operatic Ballets' designed for sense impact and simple delight. Raikes Hall Pleasure Gardens advertised the *History of the Empire* in pageant, while Mayor Bickerstaff built a half-size Eiffel Tower over Cocker's Aquarium, added a circus, sent trapeze artists swinging out over the ballroom polka-prancers and cleaned up on the whole scene.

The gypsy encampment on the South Shore where Ned and Sarah Boswell had been telling fortunes since 1836 began to extend itself to switchback rides and roundabouts. Messrs Outhwaite from Bingley, Yorkshire, and Bean from Yarmouth, Norfolk, were shortly to arrive, oust the gypsies and open an 'American-style amusement park' which they were to call the Pleasure Beach. Holland built his Ferris Wheel wherein visitors could play billiards or take high tea as they spun sedately round. Finally, the hucksters, phrenologists, palmists, quack doctors and cheapjacks who had been ushered off the beach to leave only 'ventriloquists, niggers, camels, ice cream, Blackpool rock, sweets in baskets and oyster sellers', moved into the sea-front houses, set up shop in their own front gardens and, blazing with electricity like the rest of Blackpool, bold in the face of authorities and promoters alike, brought the boozing, brawling working class firmly and finally home to roost along the Golden Mile.

Blackpool had, in fact, become a masterpiece in a certain short-lived architectural idiom. Like San Francisco or any of the frontier boom towns in the American West it was a spindly monument to rapid-fire nineteenth-century speculation. Like the frontier towns it was at the edge of the familiar world, a coastal dream city with all the speed, bustle and heady impermanence that such a position bespeaks. It was beyond the marshes, at the end of the railway, on the westerly coast, and, until amazingly late in the nineteenth-century, it was almost completely unpoliced. It echoed the World's Fair, the State Fairs, Coney Island. Networks of cables and clapboard shacks crowded round gigantic skeletal edifices. Girders sported their rows of rivets over sandy duck-boards. Big Wheel, Big Dipper, Roller Coaster, Tower overshadowed the sedate hotels, the Northerly Promenade and Park, the North Pier Indian Pavilion where ostentatious good taste could still indulge itself. Blackpool was a Lancashire coastal village that, within a man's lifetime, could turn to the South, the middle-class power nucleus, and say, 'We did it first. We lead the field in the most modern technologies, the most up-to-date entertainments, the most audacious architecture — WHAT LANCASHIRE IS DOING TODAY THE WORLD WILL BE DOING TOMORROW.' And it had by now taken on its unique identity, inheriting with that civic identity the unique double standards of the Northern music hall.

The cotton-and-coal community flocked to Blackpool week by week, each tiny black village from Preston clear to Halifax enjoying its Wakes Week by ancient custom, drawing vast sums from holiday clubs and blueing it all at Blackpool. Dave Morris could crack, in his housewife drag: 'I'm glad we're off Saturday. That Bacup lot are comin' next week' and enjoy a flood of applause from the chauvinistic neighbourhood-in-exile to which he was performing. They came first for the sea, second to gawp at the watering-place gentlefolk, thirdly to emulate the gentlefolk and finally to replace them and their culture by a powerful and ebullient style of their own. And they came to escape — escape the soot, the tedium, all the hard, deadening routine of slum life. To escape the massive permanence of authoritarian granite cities and towns. To escape work, chapel, family, the restrictive structures in which they busily scuttled like vigorous rats for the other fifty-one weeks of the year. Meeting one's neighbour in the same boarding-house one would hiss: 'Don't let on we're weavers.' The hero and heroine of *Hindle Wakes* chose their Wakes Week at Blackpool in which to significantly transgress the moral code and class stratification that so rigidly predominated at home. At Blackpool one could dance in the Tower or the Palace Ballroom, either of which was more palatial than any in London. One could see in person the cream of the entertainers who visited the local amphitheatre but once a year. One could ride in a landau, for all the world identical to the one the gaffer paraded out in of a Sunday.

And yet, at the same time, one was too close to the exposed guts of England to ignore completely the realities. One was stepping timorously out of structures and alignments on which one relied for one's very identity. No sooner had one donned one's airs and graces than one keened for the security of belonging, for the reassurance that one was surrounded by one's own sort who were all on the same game; that no one was going to notice or mind much if you did it a bit wrong, if you were wearing last year's dress, using the wrong knife and fork during those silent, edgy boarding-house breakfasts, that your assumed accent was perhaps imperfect, that the awful wear and tear the working life showed on your body and its actions showed a bit too clear.

The British working class were in steep ascendance and, from 1880 to 1945, before the privileges were won at work through growing literacy and union power, they were learned in play at Blackpool.

Blackpool did not decline with the advent of cinema that was supposed to signal the death of music hall. Nor did it decline with the war. In fact Nathaniel Gubbins suggested in his column the possibility that Blackpool had signed a private peace. Preston, Liverpool and Fleetwood blazed on either side, but Blackpool, devoid of industry, was unscathed. The London stars, including their pivotal doyen, Noël Coward, evacuated themselves to Blackpool. The entire body of the allied armed forces took their leave at Blackpool. The eating, drinking and merrymaking to be done today against tomorrow's death was being done at Blackpool under a blackout that, thanks to understanding Chief Constable Holmes, was only sketchily observed.

2

I, as the over-sensitive child of a Rochdale family transplanted to pastoral Herefordshire where the peasant culture was as red and wet and heavy as the clay, can scarcely, at this late stage, understand how fortunate I was in the fact that my mill-town parents saw fit to celebrate the end of Hostilities-in-Europe by taking their child back up the Western seaboard of the island to Blackpool. Where else to properly proclaim that the dark night was over, the Hun defeated, those Dover bluebirds clearly airborne?

In fact the first trip took place while the war was still grinding to a spluttering halt, during those limbo months between the obvious success of the Normandy invasion and the final deadening *putsch* at Hiroshima. The lights were blinking on again all over the world. The bluebirds at that stage might not be in full flight but there was blue sky for them to do it in at the end of the tunnel. The lightening load, the vast relief as the blackout lifted, could only properly be expressed by hurtling oneself into the catherine wheel of lights and riotous release at Blackpool.

And all this was despite the hampering facts that my parents were endlessly bickering about the gap between the income and the bills, about my father's scandalous extravagance in smoking twenty Players' Navy Cut a day, despite, also, both parents' ingrained teetotalism, their anxiety for a fugitive gentility they never quite managed to trap (their low income and their Northern upbringing working against them), finally despite my mother's hysterical recoil from what she called the 'low side of life'.

These very qualities had driven a dividing line between my life with them as village school teachers and my life in the dung-splattered ambience of my school friends, and it boded well to give them a bit of a hard time in the place of celebration to which they were drawn.

So off they went with me at their sleeves, trailing on, tagging on, losing them in the crowd as my shy and amazed head turned towards yet another disruptive wonder. For Blackpool had exploded in my sensibilities like a ten-tonner turned to fairy lights. Rushed out of the surrealist peace of a Herefordshire parish where the bombs had bumped for four years over the Palmeresque horizon and the harvest moon had swum in the light of distant burning cities, the bawdy, sparkling plethora of energies had swept me up in a vortex and has never quite put me down since.

The thirties were the apotheosis of the English seaside and they were the apotheosis of Blackpool. Even now the mythology of the seaside is one of the thirties, the jaunty tunes of George Formby, the characters of McGill's and Taylor's postcard comedy who are stuck with their Fred Astaire haircuts, their bobs and floral prints. The cinema, which had begun to usurp the local music hall, fed Blackpool, where there was money enough to provide that heady commodity, 'The Stars in Person'. Throughout the thirties nothing but the best was good enough for Blackpool and this carried through to the late forties with the only provision being that Blackpool might have a better idea of what was actually the best than London, Hollywood or anywhere else. The thirties and forties were a time when cinema was making sure that the popular culture was predominantly Yank. None the less, while Ted Ray, Derek Roy, and the embryonic Morecambe and Wise were perfecting their necessary mid-Atlantic accents in the shade of Abbott and Costello, the English working class, and the Northern working class in particular, exercised a strong suspicion, not to say hatred, of the American idiom. The mill town dislikes the competitive in skill and speed, preferring the honest appraisal of an honest demonstration of merit. The flash and vanity of the knut, the flapper, the wide boy, the vamp, are ridiculed in the comic-postcard tradition. It was, then, partly because of a common wish to resist the American tide that the trite, ineptly made English comedy movies of the thirties and forties enjoyed such a fanatic following. Their stars held even more box-office pull in the North of England than Hope and Crosby, because their humour was, in a number of subtle ways, native. Performers like Formby, Sandy Powell, Gracie Fields, were community heroes, figures with whom the weavers could identify, who represented the North to the world at large, and they could be seen in the flesh, in ritual splendour, at Blackpool.

Mancunian Films was the largest of a number of provincial film companies catering for this appetite. Run by John E. Blakely and his son, Tom, Mancunian Films launched most of the Northern stars, sending them off to bigger and firmer contracts. One star, however, remained with them. Initially a partner in the founding of the Manchester Studios (ironically a converted chapel and parsonage), this star remained because he didn't really care to present the North to the world. Identification ran two ways with him. Not only could a Northern audience identify with him but he so thoroughly identified with them that he remained incomprehensible to a Southern public whilst he rode on a fanatic following in the North that gave him a thousand a week which he collected (and spent) in cash, a stardom that gave him something like the privileges of Edwardian royalty and made him the undisputed king of Blackpool when that city was at the height of its combustible vitality. My parents took me to Blackpool and showed him to me.

3

The first thing my father did on arrival at Blackpool was to dump the family on the beach while he made off to 'do the bookings'. The twice nightly music-hall show had come to Blackpool rather late but the forties saw Blackpool as the capital of the idiom. Stars proliferated, their names in lights, as well as in red, white and blue print, all over every available hoarding. Off he would go and come back with a handful of pastel-shaded tickets, announce which celebrities were to be seen on which nights, so that we could relax, with our programme for the ensuing six nights mapped out before us.

At tea time, as the sea rose and that brisk wind that never quite seems to disappear from the Fylde Coast grew sharper, we would either traipse back through the quiet, strangely alien residential streets that lay behind the promenade's furore, to sit amongst the delicate pretensions of the lodging-house, or else we would queue for pie and chips and a pot of tea at one of the snack bars along the Golden Mile. After that came the show. We entered by the Dress Circle doors in sunlight and when we emerged from the Queen's, the Opera House, the Grande, the North, South or Central Piers, the city, clamorous by day, had transformed into a phantasmagoria of careening drunks, twinkling tinkling tramcars, flashing black landaus, their horses shying from the roisterous antics of reeling customers. Fairy-tale structures hung in the sky, splashing blinking light into the wet streets. Each open door spilled out a different vomit of raucous music amplified by the shrieks of unbuttoned women, fags aslant from jammy mouths, who spilled out on the arms of uniformed escorts to scream and stagger their way to call for port in the next port of call.

I am near-horizontal like a boy in a hayfield. Reginald Dixon creams out 'Now Is the Hour' (Gracie Fields's recent booty from the Maoris of New Zealand). His Wonder Wurlitzer, with its dime-novel trade lettering, displays the finest sunsets and dawns in its changing panels. I have my back on red plush exactly like that of Prince Albert's private railway carriage. I have my feet not too obtrusively stuck out on the chalky ballroom floor and I am looking up at the tumultuous vault of the Gods into which Victory has finally delivered us. I am riding a high tide of exultation which has carried me

through a late greasy supper to this apocalypse of splendour
where my parents waft fondly round the floor bestowing a
smile on me each time they pass. Their smiles drop like early
rain into a sea of bliss. I am inviolate and I am melting.

We reached the Tower Ballroom through an obstacle course
of depravity. My mother's anxiety: 'Don't look, Jeffrey. Isn't
there another way we could go, Ken?' A flight of black GIs —
'Fuggen shiyit, man.' A woman vomits, peroxide bang come
loose. Screams from the beach — 'Don't look! Don't look!' — a
pair of army-issue knickers round pale-smudge-shop-doorway
'Ooh Hank, you're smashing' thighs. And here, through the
charnel house of the flesh, through war and victory, to
something close to Heaven where I can contemplate that
turbulence of architecture and savour, item by item, the fresh
memory of the performance that has set me at such a peak of
euphoria.

The South Pier Theatre is small by Blackpool standards.
(Blackpool likes to flex its muscles, flash its wallet.) It has,
despite its finery, something of a local-hall atmosphere. It is,
in any case, Oswaldtwistle Wakes Week and the audience,
bubbling gently with anticipation of a glut of laughter, are
warming the air further by recognising neighbours across the
seat rows as the first house pours in. Anxious eyes in
tripe-and-onion faces seek the familiar along the crush in the
aisles. Frantic 'Yoo hoo' hands. Laps spill programmes,
handbags, sweets. Loud talk. Common expectations, even
concern. The man to appear is no hack, no paid *jongleur*. The
atmosphere in which he is awaited is akin to that afforded a
distinguished preacher or a union speaker. Laughter of a rare
order is owed to the audience. In return they have brought a
kind of explosive reverence. The people of Oswaldtwistle are
here and they have come to see Frank Randle.

Lights dim. Pit band, piano, drums, two saxes, two violins,
trumpet and trombone, rip into the opening medley: 'Blue
Skies', 'Driving Your Blues Away', 'Blue Skies Around the
Corner', 'Limehouse Blues'. The first half is titillatory. A pale,
austere man, later to appear as a seaside landlady, introduces
the cast with panache throughout a gathering musical tableau.
Although Randle is programmed to appear in the first half, it
is left to the king's heralds to tickle the audience's expectations
— the Kandy Sisters and Eddie, whistling Bobbie Collins, the

Three Palmers, banjo-belting Arthur Cannon, shamrock-warbling Phillip Kelly, and a whacky team of stooges led by the petticoated Gus Aubrey. An extraordinary musical aggregation called the Mandalay Choir winds up the half in sub Edward German style with a Devon landscape backdrop and Tudor cottage flats. Curtains. Then the safety drop, a collage of fascinating reading — Bile Beans, Ovaltine, Carter's Little Liver Pills, besides James Outhwaite, Eye Specialist and Countess Karamov's Herbal Remedies. More waving. The expectation intensifies.

Then, halfway through the second half (opening scenario a Deep South amalgam of *Showboat* and *Porgy and Bess* with a bit of Jolson thrown in — those ringing shouts of girls with orange knees and cobalt eyelids), as the stand-up comic Sonny Roy the Funny Boy, is winding up his act with a shaggy-dog story, a terrible head appears for a moment through the curtains. It is like the cuckoo from the cuckoo clock, the court jester in the guillotine, wild of eye and manic of demeanour, wrought from spiritual elements of the hen-run and the madhouse, a strutting, crowing geriatric, an eminence gone boneless with bubbling libido from which controlling sanity has been for ever lifted. And, as this touchpaper sparks from behind the gagster's carefully oblivious shoulder, the charge of gelignite that has been straining its boundaries danger-ously in the bellies and lungs, the corsets and BVDs, the family groups and the neighbourhood knots, throughout the amphitheatre, explodes with a sustained roar fit to crack the heavens.

The laughter dies but, an infinitesimal shade of a second before the theatre has completely settled to rest, the head waggles as though jolted by some violent impulse of randiness injected from whatever fabulous forms of animated decrepi-tude are concealed by the drapes. The eyes roll like pickled eggs loose in brine and one precipitate menopausal cackle from somewhere around the fourth row of the stalls sends the whole cloud up again, billowing and bellowing, discharging small side-explosions of recognition and solidarity — 'Nathen, Frank, coom on y'owd bugger.'

And then the head freezes (Sonny Roy the Funny Boy become straight-man is still suspended in mid-narrative under the mike), completely inactive. The theatre awaits its next tremor with the breathless anticipation a trapeze act normally commands. What will he do? What will he say?

The head is taken by a second convulsion as though shaking off the residue of the first, and this lifts the laughter-cloud again. Then the head is gone, leaving the cloud inflated, echoing and booming.

Sonny Roy the Funny Boy lets it settle. He finishes his story cleverly, using Randle's unforgivable upstaging as a piece of suspense in his own long joke. Telescoping the narrative cleverly he winds up in two short sentences and a monosyllabic punch-line that makes use of the laughter Randle has left on the boil. But he makes it the finish of his act. The quarry has been glimpsed and now no one must stand between the audience and their idol.

Unlike Formby at the Opera House, who, in the tradition of that theatre, makes great use of spectacle, Randle needs very little besides his body with its grotesque head.

The front curtain goes up amidst dense silence on a backdrop where a Sunny Scene complete with village inn and signpost has been baldly painted. Where is he? Will he really enter? What will he do when he appears?

The hero's coming is announced by a slow, steady thump, something like the knocking of a malevolent ghost. Each blow is spaced with crafty irregularity so that it bangs out just before or slightly after it's expected, teasing, rib-tickling, warming the expectations once again to unbearable intensity.

And he appears CLUMP. Decrepit, revolting, irrepressible CLUMP. Clinging to a rough-cut tree branch higher than his own head CLUMP. A pair of khaki shorts as baggy and decrepit as a wet bell tent, hung over a pair of knees like billiard balls. Ragged muffler. Baggy jacket. Hair standing up from his bald pate in a kind of cock's comb. *Pince-nez* perilous on his nose. A rucksack as inflated as the balloon of humour with which he so skilfully juggles. From a pocket like a sack juts the black screw-cap of a beer flagon. On his boneless face he wears an audible smile, his mouth stretched under his nose to emit a constant octogenarian gurgle which acts as a bridge from gag to gag like the drone knits the phrases of a bagpipe. Somewhere deep in that abominable head indecent juices are bubbling compounded of challenge, exultation, scepticism, libido, and a defiant sense of the absurdity of his own enviable vitality. Their subtle eruption in that scraggy throat constitutes the formation of the Lancashire 'Eeee'. A randy pawing of the ground is indicated, a chortling faith in one's own unkillable spirit — 'Eeee, I'll gi'e 'em some stick!'

And his rolling eye, his out-thrown torso, his bandy, stomping deportment say: 'Here I am. What do you think of me? Aren't I amazing?'

'Eeeeee Oswaldtwistle,' he exults through the rising laughter. The name of the town that is present in force is something of a gift for Randle. The resounding 's's and 't's bring those gurgling juices to his flabby lips where they spray out like sparklers into the stage lights. He is full of subtle foretastes of the excess everyone knows is to come. There he stands, as abominable and hilarious as everybody's wildest imaginings, extravagant, unbelievable, but plain as a toper's nose for all to see. His first gag then is about this audacious display. 'Baghum, A seez a kid up theer, come runnin' to 'iz mother. "Come 'ere mother, thur'z a monkey up a stick!"' Proud of it, too. Like the piece of tree he holds in his fist, an emblem, a totem, a chapstick.

The throat gurgle finds somewhere in its stave a dying whine of resignation. 'Aye — Eeee. Wellaye, eeee . . .', skilfully scored into the tenor of the laughter. Fatalistically, a fact that one can take or leave. 'A've walked through Europe, Earup, Ireup, Wallop, Jollop, aye. . . .' The rising cadenza of lip-popping 'p's dissolves again into the laughter that never quite dies. The cloud is kept off the ground, never settles . . .

'Me feet are reddott! But baghum A've just 'ad a bit of a narra squeak.' The 'e' sound allows him to stretch his lips near to the back of his neck. The 'k' clacks out. The orchestration of his patter is gurgle, against sudden shouted statement, dying into an innuendo that is kicked out of the way by savagely emphasised syllables. 'A wozz goon' across a *field*. Thur woz a bull innit. It wozn't Barney's bull neither . . . aye . . .' dying into a complicity with the audience who acknowledge the reference to a mutual myth by sending the cloud up to the ceiling again. 'In fact it woz an 'ell of a long way from bein' Barney's bull!' Voice dies again, 'Aye. . . .', into the laughter. 'Ooooooo it woz a fierce un! It 'ad a coupla prongs on it az long az this stick.' The sudden angle of the displayed tree tickles that surprised female shriek from the stalls. He teases her

response with a mock-threatening jab. Woman stifles her
helpless giggles for very shame but the ripples spread. '. . .
only they were a damn sight sharper ner this, I'll tell yer. It
come tuppin' away . . .', gurgle into sigh again, giving the
word 'away' a curious *double entendre*. 'A thowt it woz
apologizin', the way it woz bowin' and scrapin' away . . .',
rides the laughter with an extended 'Aye . . . Aye, A shooed it
away wi' me 'andkerchief . . .', brandishes huge red spotted
bandana, rides laugh with a knowing, grinding 'Aye. . .'. By
now the theatre has difficulty restraining its laughter
sufficiently to hear the next line. Each emphasised syllable is
underlined with a pawing of the ground with his great boot
which he wears on the wrong foot, by a spasm of the knees;
each dying drone is accompanied by a 360 degrees survey of the
auditorium, manipulating the direction and the warmth of the
rapport. Randle plays his visual tricks with a restraint that
subtly contradicts his obvious extravagance. There is the power
in him to precipitate total hysteria. He has plenty of margin to
play with and he deploys it sparingly. 'It med it a damn sight
wuss . . . aye . . . aye. . . . It come, but did I pick 'em up? A
furly sizzled!' 'Z's buzz waspishly. The immediate picture of this
bag of impudent senility haring across a field pursued by a bull
with clouds of wrath snorting from either nostril, a simple
image straight from the pen of the *Film Fun* cartoonist who, at
that time, had Randle as a strip character, keeps the cloud up
and bouncing. 'A catched up a rabbit!. . . A'd 'a' passed it
only it got between me legz. . . . A sed to it, "Eh, come on,
'urry up or else get out o't' rooid." A sed, "Let somebody run
as con"' and the dialect vowel, 'can' to 'con', releases a
dangerous explosion of humour which is becoming increasingly nothing more than a celebration of complicity.
'Eeeeee,' he gurgles. 'Eeeee . . . Hikerz? Hikerz? A've picked
'em off t' bushez. . . . A'm the daddy of all hikerz. I'll be 82 in
a few more days. Eighty-two and A'm as full of vim az a
butcher'z dog. . . . A'm as livelagh' — last syllable of 'lively' is
a belch carefully supressed and used to change the tone of the
vowel — 'az a cricket. Why, A'll tek anybody hon at me age
and weight — dead or alive. . . .' The laughter balloon, let to
rest a bit, gets a prod. 'An' A'll run 'em, walk 'em, jump 'em,
fight 'em . . . aaaa — a — aghye. . . .' An extended sighing
drone implies the missing alliterative syllable and the laughter

cloud is inflated to the full again. There is little point to what the hero is saying now. The lines, rather than being jokes, are love-catalysts convincing the people of Oswaldtwistle yet more that he is an amazing old goat and is veritably one of them. Final deflatory line to his sporting challenge: 'An' A'll play 'em dominoez. . . .' The 's' turns into a cascading raspberry. 'Mind you, I attribute me excellent 'ealth to moderation, exercize, plenty o' fresh urr. . . .' Pause. 'A gooz t' bed early an' A gooz t' sleep. . . .' Touching on the (then) unmentionables and touching the tender part in the giggle-organs of the lady in the stalls. Fixes her with a ferocious eye. 'Thur'z no monkey bizness about me. A' — dyspeptically extended — 'A — a — agh'll tell yi. . . . Eeeeh . . . 82 and just look at these for a pur o' legz.' Desporting again his cartoon image. 'A tossed a sparra for these an' lost.'

The verbal structure of the act is gradually being discarded. The balloon is sustained increasingly by underlining of character, by visuals and aurals. It is a subtle reassurance for the bottom levels of the working class, the heavy manual labourers who are uncomfortable with words most of the time. It is a warm collective return to the infantile with all the consonant dropping of taboos — 'Baghum, thur'z another hurr comin' 'ere' — seizes it between finger and thumb and pulls the hair out straight so that a tiny peak of stretched flesh is visible. The sight is simultaneously outrageous and relieving. The owd bugger is actually playing with his body like a child, and so, we feel, might we. The implications are obvious but never stated. 'Eeeee well. A goo t' Buckabury!' — approximation to 'buggery', then unthinkable on stage or in print. His hand explores the awful regions of his thigh, overhung by his vast shorts. How far will the exploration extend. Will he? Dare he? He meets the challenge with a saucy, quizzical glare. 'Thur's a hurr 'ere wi' a knot in it . . . aye . . . aye. . . . It'z surprisin' wur thi keep comin' from. Eighty two an' look at this for a thick 'urr. . . .' High enough now for dangerous *double entendre*. The lady in the stalls obliges. Turns towards the poor shrieking creature whose bladder must, by now, be totally abandoned, displays the distended growth with all the phallic air of a bantam. 'Straight as a bulrush!' — biblical use of rhetoric, driving the *double entendre* ruthlessly home. And now that sex has been filtered into the range of reference

Randle knows that he has activated a whole new set of raw nerves. Like Max Miller he has a thorough knowledge of, and to some extent shares, all the repressions and double standards of a class whose sex is severely discoloured by large families in two-room terrace houses, by the systematic guilt-policies of the Methodist and Baptist movements, by the incapacity following fatigue after ten- and twelve-hour shifts. Each nerve in this new category is swollen to hypersensitivity by hot compression of guilt and the longing for release. He is further into the region of the seaside postcard. He approaches the 'saucy'.

'A just passed a coupla tartz ont' rooid yonder. Eeee, thi were a coupla hottunz!' Catch-phrase there, one of the three or four he used. The balloon, fallen a little in anticipation, rises again. 'He — heeee! One of 'em went like this 'ere t' me. Hehee . . . aye . . .' Long, wild mime as the eyes revolve and distort in a burlesque of a vamp's come-hither look. 'Aye . . . but A took n' notice . . . *much!* A sed to 'er, A sed "Not today, luv. A'd rayther 'ev a Kensitas!"', Use of current cig-ad slogan expressing (warmly approved) immunity to sex. The biggest laugh of the night so far, the cloud near bursting, lifting the roof slightly.

'Well A woz 'evvin' a bit o' fun wi' these youngunz. A took one of 'em for a walk. We walked about five miles. Neither of us spoke a word. A sed, "A penny for yer thoughts." Ooo she gimme such a clout across t' lug. A sed, "Wot's t'do wi' yi? I only sed a penny for yer thoughts." "Ee," she said. "A thowt yi sed a penny for me shorts."' The gurgle in full spate carries through the huge gust of laughter. And now to the bottle: 'A think A'll 'ev a sup. Aye. . . .' He gargles. Here come the great inevitables of every Randle performance. 'All slops!' he pronounces — play on brewery trade name Allsops — and then he belches formidably. 'Baghum, yi'll 'ave to excuse . . .' but he's overtaken by another eruption and now, at its most gastric, simple, alimentary, explicit point, Randle's style is at its purest. Now the audience knows that the spoken word may be abandoned. Some may be getting ready to miss evening meals or last buses. They have seen him at their home-town halls with his own troup, Randle's Scandals. They have heard the indomitable Gus Aubrey announce him, seen the spot strike the left-hand wings and have to swing across to find Randle dressed in God-knows-what amazing apparel, waving a

beer flagon and gurgling, and they know that huge cloud of
laughter can be kept up there in the smoky dome of the theatre
for hours, literally hours, after the script has run out. They
know that this monkey-up-a-stick can, if the mood takes him
and if the alcohol is raging correctly in his blood, prolong the
show until the orchestra has gone and there's no one left to
play the King. For they know in their ticklish ribs that it is no
more than the placing of a movement or the twitch of a limb,
no more than the lyric gurgling of this bewitched ale-drain
that is needed to weld the theatre into some terrible dense
custard of class solidarity.

But on this occasion he is on good behaviour. Due measure
is given but the tidy shape of the show observed. Jack Taylor,
the producer, has in fact his name emblazoned in lights
outside and there has, this season, been trouble enough.

'Baghum,' says Randle, scrutinising the amber swill within,
'it'z some sharp stuff, iz this ale. Baghum, it'z all armz and
legz. Thur'z no body innit.' The cloud rolls. 'A sed t' landlord
o' t' pub wur A gottit, A sed, "It'z a bit thin, this, mister."
"Aye," 'e sed. "You'd be thin if you'd come up the same pipes
as this ale 'az. Aye," 'e sed, "A bet yi've never tasted owt
better." A sed, "No but A've paddled about in it."' Complicity
again, the brotherhood of the twenty-pint day and the blocked
drain, cemented with a vast belch like rending metal.

'Aye . . .' cooling it again. 'A don't like theze booitz. A'm
brekkin 'em in for me father. . . . Thu're gein' me corns a bit
o' gyp t'dee. . . . A woz troubled wi' a corn. A went t'
chiropoddle, Dr Scollops. . . . 'E 'ed a look. 'E sed, "Baghum
owd lad, yi've got some mucky feet." A sed, "Ur thi muckier
than thine?" 'E sed, "Thi urr that." A sed, "Well don't forget,
A'm a lot older than thee, y'know!. . . . A sed, "Nathen, wot
about this corn?" 'E sed, "Thur'z no corn theer." It woz a collar
stud in me sock. Three weeks A'd been in pain. . . . Aye. . . .'

A vast belch: 'A don't like this ale but A'll sup it if it keeps
me up all neet' — back in the filth, working up to the finish.
'Thur'z about thirty-six burps in this bottle' — another catch
phrase that gets a huge recognition. 'Eeee that just remindz
me. A wonce sent a bottle of beer like this hawee t' be
analaysed. Thi must 'ave got mixed up at t'other end. Thi sent
me a postcard sayin', "Dear Sir, Your 'orse iz in perfect
condition."'

And that's it. Up goes the laughter, the huge buffeting cloud, and then down it comes, gently down. 'Eeeeaye, A can rattle me dogs about a bit y'know. But it's only me bit o' fun. Don't tek any notice o' me. A'm just an owd fooil, that'z all. An' if you tek my advice now, all you young unz — ' — Even a serious note now? — A moral? — 'A'm owd enough t' mek most of yerz grandfather — Get plenty of exercise, plenty of fresh urr and ale. Look at me. A'm 82. A could jump a five-bar gate — if it woz laid ont' floor like. . . .' — the fading note — 'It woz only t'other dee. A went to a funeral. A woz comin' awee from t' graveside. A chap looks at me, 'e sez, " 'Ow old are you?" A sed, "82." 'E sed, "A don't think it's much use you goin' 'ome at all. . . ." '

The tree plant strikes up again. The applause fills the theatre like white sound. The clumping stick punctuates his exit and he leaves us fed, well fed, replete. An hour later I gaze into the scrambled Olympian ceiling of the Tower Ballroom, indulged in a special warmth of well-being, of belonging to the human species, and Frank Randle has given it to me.

My mother, who had laughed herself to a mass of jelly, thought he went too far. This was significant.

PART II

A Very Very Funny Man

1

The British Music Hall Society sent me a card with a bright charity stamp on it. I was quite proud of it. I hung it on my office wall at the Art School, a connection with a robust world that others might envy. It said that my query had been passed on to their information secretary who would be getting in touch with me.

'That's in the bag, then,' I said to myself. 'These old kids will come home with all the gen.' Don Ross, the Josephs had mentioned. If he was the information officer I would doubtlessly be very thoroughly informed.

Nothing happened and I started to flap. Somebody gave me the addresses of a couple of pubs near Burnley. Contacts. Relatives perhaps. I wrote but nobody wrote back.

Frank Randle seemed to be insulated by an impenetrable wall. There was something behind the reluctance to speak. 'Always reliable with us,' Stanley Joseph had said. With whom, then, was he not reliable? What was the scandal? The irony I didn't, at that time, comprehend.

Time was wearing down. It was just before Christmas that, having resigned from the post of Chairman of the National Poetry Society in disgust, I found John Fisher's book, *A Funny*

Way To Be a Hero, newly in Paladin Paperback. There was another irony there but it would be self-indulgent to describe it. Fisher had a chapter on Randle. I was impatient and phoned him after having written. There was a letter coming he said, and there was. There was a Randle widow, he said. His old hardback publishers had had a copyright hassle. They might shine the way. And there was a man called Buttery at Manchester BBC who had worked as an editor for the Mancunian Film Corporation. Don Ross, he confirmed, was the best man to see at the British Music Hall Society.

I rang the Variety Club of Great Britain by mistake. They were mainly a charity organisation, they said. That seemed to tie up with the charity stamp on the card, but it didn't. Finally I got the British Music Hall Society. A mildly confused but helpful lady said her dad was out. She gave me a number for Don Ross. Brighton.

Ross's voice, over the phone, had a very particular accent, not BBC, not cockney, not Jewish, particularly, but a front-of-house accent with a certain friendly distancing, the dignity of the Homburg hat.

'I knew Frank Randle when he was one of the Bouncing Randles, a trampoline act. Frank Randle was a very very funny man.'

And nobody had ever said he wasn't. Against what were these testimonies of merit arraigned?

What was the secret, I asked. What inspired these cautiously defensive tones?

'Well,' said Ross, 'it's because of the totally wild things he did.'

What things? 'Well, I was at the Liverpool Empire with *Thanks for the Memory*.' I vaguely remembered a road show of Edwardian troupers ushered back into the limelight. 'I thought, having got the show staged, I'd just have time to nip across to the Pavilion where Randle was playing, and see him, then nip back in time for second half. Well, when I got there he was very pleased to see me, very pleased indeed. "Hello Don," he said. "Look, I'm on in a minute. There's a crate of Guinness there. Don't go till I get back. I'll keep it short." Well, I knew Frank once he got on stage so I drank my drink, looked at my watch and thought, "I must be going." But I couldn't go. I couldn't leave. The bugger had locked me in.'

'And so you stayed?'

'Yes, and I was needed back at the Empire. That was Frank you see. He didn't give a damn. There was another time — '

'Yes?'

'Yes — I was in Liverpool again and I noticed that Frank was on at the Empire. Well, I thought, I'll just nip round and say hello to old Frank. But when I got there the doorman, he wouldn't let me in. "Nobody," he said, "nobody comes backstage but members of the cast."

'"But I'm Don Ross," I said. "I'm a personal friend of Mr Randle. I been in show business for — "

'"Nobody comes backstage but members — " Well, at that moment I saw Frank at the end of the corridor. "Frank," I said. "They won't let me in."

'"Of course they'll let you in. Look," he said to the doorman, "this is Don Ross, a personal friend of mine."

'"I'm sorry Mr Randle," says the doorman, "but it's a rule of the theatre. Nobody comes — "

'"Listen," says Randle. "Either he comes in or I don't go on. You can take your pick." And he wouldn't have. I got in. He was like that you see. Didn't give a damn.'

'Loyal, though.'

'Oh, if he liked you, loyal to a fault.'

I asked if I could come and see him. He said he had nothing else to tell me so there was no point. I said my thank yous. 'A great comedian,' said Ross. 'A very very funny man.'

Buttery answered my letter. He suggested a number of contacts. Tom Blakely, the son of John E. Blakely who used to run Mancunian Films, lived somewhere in Wilmslow. Directory Enquiries gave me his number. Yes, he knew Randle well. Would I like to come round? We fixed a date a week hence and, on a morning when fog, belting rain and the entire fleet of British container-delivery lorries were battling it out across the Pennines, Petal levered me into her rusty minivan and drove me first to Saddleworth for a snort, and thence, after two million wrong turns, to Wilmslow.

The M62, like all motorways, keeps you in concrete. On either hand you can see the old black scars of the nation's function, the meandering roads, the gappy, fallen walls, bridle paths, pack-horse tracks, gently smoking mills, decrepitude, decay, residue of hard practice, crude necessity. There goes

Bradford, Brighouse, Huddersfield, over there Halifax. Rochdale in the distance. Oldham on the left. Ten million people; twenty generations; a thousand or two fortunes made and lost. The guts and the arsehole of a nation's power passed in seconds. A touch of a calfskin shoe to a rubber-capped pedal and the concrete mentality can reduce all this scabby drama to its proper irrelevance, can make of it no more than a movie, a visual *obbligato* to the rock gobbling out of the cassette recorder built into the leatherbound dashboard. Concrete enables one to move. Involvement hampers the concrete world. Insulate your living space. Pay your car park by computer. Never get out of your car. Only stop where the credit card's flashed. Roots are anathema. Hate roots.

Off the motorway, down into Saddleworth, the twisting road slows you down to human scale. The concrete functionaries who work the new office blocks in Manchester have come here to pretend humanity. Human contact is a status symbol, like Morris chairs and tin kettles. The weavers' cottages have yellow doors and carports. Fitted carpets cover the bar parlour flags. If the flags are bare it's for the wine-bar touch.

Nobody knows the way in concrete land. You follow the signs. The signs are simple and unambiguous. Never any shades of direction, no alternative routes, no well-loved lanes or familiar corners. Choice. Decide where you're going and go there, this way or that. Get in your lane now. Finer shades of intuition could get you smashed to death. The issues are child-simple. Be a child. Don't grow. Can't anyway. No roots. Hate 'em.

North of Manchester the motorways work themselves into a scramble. The hurtling cavalcade has to be sifted, sorted, directed to Bolton, Blackburn, Preston, Liverpool, Manchester Airport, Lancaster and Scotland, Chester and Wrexham, Huddersfield and Leeds. In places eight lanes cruise their speedy way under the overhead directions with menacing calm. What of Oldham, Darwen, Burnley? Robbed of their identity as being '*en route*' to anywhere, they snooze their way into insignificance, mildly mollified by their new concrete shopping centres.

One of the motorways is a go-nowhere *cul-de-sac* that whistles you down through Manchester's western suburbs to Cheshire, where the guts of Britain find their boundary.

Petal tools her decrepit banger into the sedate streets of Wilmslow. The knot of rubber monsters hanging in a collective embrace from her driving mirror bounces with no small air of irony. Out of Wilmslow, take the Knutsford Road at the roundabout. Then turn left.

The district is suddenly contrivedly rural. The road is unadopted, as rough as a tank track. Petal's banger, weak of spring and smooth of tyre, crashes merrily along between bungalows spread across discreet lawns. There is wrought iron and some topiary. Cardiganed figures stoop their slippered way to the net curtains and look out on Petal's lurching sardine can of a car.

She dumps me outside 18 Cobbing's Lane, then crashes back to Wilmslow to buy sweeties.

Tom Blakely is kind, welcoming and sleek. His house, his demeanour, his pretty little wife, bespeak a careful attention to modest but expensive pleasures. The man's style constitutes a wish to demonstrate a personal and selective cultivation of the comforts of retirement. He, like the watchbirds all along the drive, wears cardigan and good leather slippers. He is not particularly overweight. There is a photograph on the sideboard of someone getting wed who I take to be his son. The young man looks a bit like Rolf Harris.

My decrepit mackintosh having been taken and hung somewhere, the introductory niceties about weather, journey and wrong turnings having been properly observed, we settle down to the interview over home-made sponge cake and tea in fine china. Mrs Blakely, blonde in a very taking Chinese dress, sits silently in attendance, twinkling sufficiently to banish any air of subservience.

'Randle made nine films with my father and I'd be willing to bet there are only two remaining. I've got 'em. We sold the others to Butcher's in London and I'm almost certain they've junked 'em.'

'Your father?'

'Yes, John E. Blakely.'

'What did you do?'

'Oh, I was manager. Business manager. Sometimes stage manager. General administrator. We made George Formby's first films and then we worked with Randle. Randle, I may tell you, was a very very funny man.'

Blakely is proud of Mancunian Films. There was no doubt about it, they were wartime shoestring jobs — a grand example of local initiative plunging into any territory of speculation with an exuberant optimism we are all unfortunate enough to have grown out of. In style and technique their primitive directness are almost classic. Peter Wright had written a book called *Laughter in the Rain* but a copy had never appeared. Tom Blakely tells me how much money the films made. A hell of a lot.

Blakely is sure that Randle was born in Wigan. He was always a gentleman offstage, quiet, reserved. 'We never saw any evidence of wild behaviour. Never too drunk to work. Always a glass in his hand but certainly not alcoholic. Do you remember, dear? Mind you, he would disappear for days. No warning. Just turn up at the studios at 8 o'clock and no Randle.' Where did he go? Who knows? Possible mental blackouts, fits of depression. Possible benders with Joe Locke. Did I know that Randle and Joe Locke were friendly? I would do well to contact Joe Locke. Those strained fragments from light opera I remember wafting from the wartime wireless sort uneasily with the idea of two- and three-day benders. And there was maybe a girlfriend somewhere. Tom and his wife exchange smiles. 'But he had a lovely house, you know, in Whitegate Drive, Blackpool, and a lovely wife, Queenie. We loved Queenie, didn't we dear?'

Mrs Blakely smiles, still a little mischievous. 'Mind you, Randle could be hell to work with. Not to my father. We understood him, you see. If he disappeared we just waited till he turned up. And he could never stick to a script so we'd go through the formality of attempting the script, then he'd turn to my father and say "Can I make it up now Dada?" — That's what they all called him, Dada — "Can I make it up now, Dada?" and off he'd go. But other stars — I remember one day Tessie O'Shea came in the office in floods of tears, and she was a tough one, Tessie. "That bastard Randle," she said.'

'What had he done?'

'Oh, he'd told her that she wasn't any good. She'd never be a great performer. He was like that you see, unpredictable. And there was the occasion with Diana Dors. He hated Diana Dors. Mind you she was a bad girl, she and her first husband. A very naughty girl in those days.'

La Dors had been reluctant to honour her contract on finding that her co-star in *It's a Grand Life* was not in any way describable as swinging, that she had, in fact, signed up to film with a veritable lion of the lumpen, the lowest comic the low-class North could produce. Tom had had to show a little bit of legal muscle to get her up to the studios. Randle knew this and seized his opportunity of kicking her in the gut the first day. For that is where La Dors felt the megrims and the vapours on the first day's filming. Randle dashed out to the off-licence for medicine. The medicine was as many concentrated short drinks as he could get into a tumbler (that Nothern use of booze as a test and a lever of character). La Dors was out of action for three days. 'That's someone you should talk to, Diana Dors.'

'Difficult Randle was, unpredictable, but well liked and basically a gentleman. Mark you, there was the incident with the pistol. . . .'

I should see a Mr Brennan, the brother of the great Northern promoter Jimmy Brennan. They had owned the Queen's Theatre, Blackpool and the brother still ran the Brennan Cinema Circuit. And Dan Young, one of Randle's fellow comics, I should see, and Tessie O'Shea. And there is a man around Manchester claiming to be Randle's son, it seems. A painter called Arthur Delaney. That was Randle's real name, Delaney. Mrs Blakely has seen some of Arthur Delaney's paintings in a gallery at Alderley Edge. Maybe if I went along now. . . .

Petal returns from the shops looking, as usual, like a small and vulnerable beast. She takes tea and we depart. As we go Petal spills her peppermints all over the front drive.

The gallery in Alderley Edge is one sneeze off a mirror shop. The paintings are corny and saleable, fresh, locally painted. Landscapes. Interiors. Flowers. Delaney has a number on display and they are about the best in stock. Chunky, bright little pictures, well made, with a strong Lowry influence.

The proprietor is affable behind his sporty bow tie, under his suede trilby. 'About Randle? Arthur will be delighted. I've been trying to ring him all day. I'll give him another try now.'

And suddenly the enquiry is under way. I am on the phone to the actual son of Frank Randle, a man who, if he's willing, is surely able to strip away all shrouds, explain all contradictions. Perhaps I shall really have my talisman in detail.

Who was I? What did I want? Did I realise he had an evening engagement? It was only chance that I'd got him. Did I realise how busy he was? That he's left the phone off the hook all day in order to get on with his painting? Wildly I hit on a question to cut through the formalities of reluctance. When did Randle die? What of?

And the dark squibs start to come through, the secret family facts, charged with terror-energies and magic.

Gastro-enteritis. At his home in Blackpool. Suffered from TB for six years, secretly innoculating himself with strepto-mycin. A bottle and a half of whiskey a day, at least. 'It's a long, sad tale. Anyway who are you? Jeff who?'

I get the number and, with slight difficulty, the address. No, tonight is out of the question. He has, as he has explained, an engagement. Half way between Alderley Edge and Wilmslow we get a flat tyre.

2

Delaney is as good as his word. He is seldom or never home and, if he is, his phone is off the hook. Eventually, on Saturday night, he answers. After a bit of conversational skirmishing he asks me how old I am. Forty-three I reply, hand on heart. I saw his father at Blackpool when I was a kid. The whole operation is a labour of love, I am certainly no hack trying to rake muck. I am not trying to paint a black picture.

'A black picture is what it is though, I'm afraid. . . .'

'There's something no one will tell me about your father.'

'Yes,' says Delaney. 'I'm it. You'd better come and see me.'

I put ads in the *Stage* and write a letter to the *Guardian*. A lot of ringing around after Locke, Nat Jackley, Sandy Powell, Tessie O'Shea, Diana Dors has got me next to nowhere. BBC, agencies, theatre managements, by some long-established freemasonry of the profession, protect the privacy of entertainers, even long-retired entertainers, as savagely as they would protect their own progeny. The *Blackpool Gazette* publishes a request for information but the *Guardian* doesn't publish that kind of letter, they tell me. They pass my letter on to Stephen Dixon, their art critic, who admits to being a nostalgia freak. He suggests all the old troupers I'm already on the track of, provides addresses for one or two and tells me that Jim Casey, son of Jimmy James, possibly the greatest comedian of all time, is working for Manchester BBC. It's to be Delaney and Casey in one day, then. With a hip flask in the glove compartment and Petal resolute at the wheel the vibrator hits the M6 once again.

Albert Square looks as fine as ever despite concrete encroachments. The road leads out under the railway bridge into the totally concrete realms of the University, the home of the Renaissance Theory of Technology, numeracy and literacy ideas of education, the central academic computer and Professor Cox. Not only is the architecture purest Dusseldorf but here the rationalisation of concrete is most predominant. Here are the protagonists of centrality, unity and gaga nursery-rhyme simplicity of reason. The residue of the nineteenth-century festering all around these cooling towers is not even an irritation. Outside the paradigm, it doesn't even exist. Was that a belligerent little man in a cream-coloured Jaguar sports model who just overtook us at 90 waving a bottle of Guinness?

Peaceville Road is opposite a vast, unpleasant Berni Inn. I wonder wildly how the nationwide monopolies — Bass-Charrington, MacFisheries, Trust Houses Forte, Mecca, Granada, Berni Inns — might betoken a growing national sanity in the minds of Messrs Eysenek and Skinner. Peacehaven is, anyway, a little haven of 1930s subtopia. A flashy sports model with exposed plumbing and trumpet horns all polished to a perfect finish stands outside Number 2.

Arthur Delaney is balding, middle-aged and pink in more than just the visual sense. He welcomes us in and tells Petal how to find the Whitworth Art Gallery. Like Blakely, he regards the interview as a job of work and is anxious to get down to it.

We sit down to tea and cake. There is a magnificent Western saddle on its tree in the corner, a bronze bust of Lowry wearing real gold rim spectacles by the record player, a signed photograph of Bing Crosby lined up with Delaney's own best canvasses on the wall. The house is a bit chilly but no one seems to mind. Delaney has a mildly obsessive man's imperviousness to minor discomfort.

I recall the telephone conversation. 'I'll tell you the position y'see,' says Delaney. 'Well, we've 'ad a private side to our lives — Me mam and dad.' The face wreathes itself into a mass of complicit difficulty. 'They were never married y'see, and that's the whole core of the thing and I — ' — the pause underlines the loaded nature of the information — ' — was brought up by a stepfather. Now in respect for that man, a smashin' bloke, a good stepfather — he's dead now — we've always kept a low profile on this — y'know.'

I affirm that I do in fact know.

'And me mother's alive although she's in 'ospital because she 'ad a stroke years ago. Y'know, we just let that lie y'see.'

'Your stepfather was married to your actual mother?' I say, tact and nervous whiskey nips leaving my intellect somewhere back along the M6.

'Yes,' says Arthur Delaney.

'I see,' says Jeff Nuttall.

'But,' he goes on, 'she lived — ' Then he stops. 'Arthur McEvoy was me father's name — '

'Arthur McEvoy? Oh. Better make a note of that because somebody misinformed me, then.'

'Okay. What've they told yi?'

'They told me his real name was Frank Delaney.'

'It was Arthur McEvoy.'

'Oh.'

'And that's my name. I only used Delaney from being 21 years old, which was me mother's stage name.'

'Your mother was on the stage?'

'Yes, yes. That's where she met 'im. She was a sister act. They were three sisters, me Auntie Bennie, me Auntie Mona and me mam, Eva; and the two younger ones were me mother and Auntie Mona. They 'ad a double act, Delaney and Lee but they were real sisters. The real name was Willis, and the elder sister was established in the business with an act called the Veldons and Harry Friend, and she married two or three times. Y'know show business.'

Smiles of understanding.

'I 'ate t' tell yi, it's so complicated. And she died only a few months ago. And 'er second 'usband, Jack Greaves — he was a comedian right to retiring — he's 80-odd now, very bright and intelligent and y' don't want to, y'know, bring anything else of the — Y'know, they've all got skeletons in the cupboard, y'know. . . .'

Jack Greaves is shortly to join the ranks of his deceased colleagues (Some dress-circle bar where these rusty voiced troupers sit over their celestial gin? Let's hope so, at least. . . .) but neither of us know that just yet.

With a mouthful of home-made cake, I offer to exclude mention of Arthur or indeed any relatives from the account, but Arthur, skeletal or not (and sitting on his leatherbound settee across the coffee table, he doesn't look very skeletal), is anxious to be included. He is, after all, the only child in a kind of royal lineage. He was, anyway, on good terms with his dad. A kind of protective pride begins to be discernable as the predominant tone of the interview. Delaney knows that I am going to break into some sordid corners but he is anxious that I should have a good solid concept of the humanity, even the nobility, of his father. He had known who his real father was since he came of age, but not before. 'Er — well — when I was a little boy I didn't know, because he was Arthur Twist then. He worked on the horizontal bars. He was on the trampoline. . . .'

Arthur McEvoy, then, had become Arthur Twist and Arthur Twist had become Frank Randle — 'There was an advert. I don't know if it was mustard, but there was somethin', Randle's mustard, condiments or somethin'. 'E said "I might as well just call meself Randle" — y'know, and that's always been his name. Eva liked it. As for Arthur to Frank, well, nobody who's called Arthur likes the name. No. Arthur's like — er — dependable, stodgy, kind of Alberty — like "Our Arthur", y'know. . . .'

There was never any Bouncing Randles, Arthur believes. He also believes that before Frank joined the show with Eva Delaney he had been a collier. Delaney is most defensive about mis-information. He clearly goes by first-hand experience and by his mother's memories. He is leery of trade journalists and the gossip of old pros. 'Rubbish,' he says. 'I think I'd better just tell you what the real story is.'

The story he unrolls is one of drunken violence, colossal idealism, paranoia, megalomania, bad marriage — 'She came

in a show, Queenie. I don't know which show it was but she was
with like an act like the Luton Girls' Choir. They were pros but
they were a quiet act — he wanted a lady and to him she *was* a
lady, and she *was* a lady, by the way. Put that on record. She
was a lovely woman.' . . . A tale of disease, illicit unrequited
love, and finally of a miserable death, and he tells the whole sad
tale sheathed in a quality of the most profound respect. The
discovery of Uncle Arthur's real identity when he came of age.
Long, boozey chats in musty dressing rooms. Hurtling night
drives over cobbled streets and tram lines.

The lid is coming off. The secrets are emerging and I am
finding that Randle's ghost, which I am pursuing with my own
curious romantic reverence, is protected by something far
stronger than professional protocol. I wonder if he knew, as he
stormed, swilled and smashed his way about show business,
just how well-loved he obviously was. Gus Aubrey will tell
me a good tale or two. Gus was the main stooge. He works in a
shop in Manchester somewhere. Another person I should
look up is Randle's *bête noire*, Blackpool police chief, Harry
Barnes.

Arthur winds up with a story that most closely expresses the
tone in which the interview has taken place. The father of the
Willis girls was a fine old Edwardian comic called Billy Willis.
Taken feeble in his old age Billy had to be sent to a
happy-valley home somewhere. Money was forthcoming
because Arthur Twist a.k.a. Frank Randle had paid a weekly
donation towards Arthur Delaney's keep all Arthur Delaney's
life, and because Genevieve Willis a.k.a. Eva Delaney had
never, in her typical pride, ever touched a penny of it.

Petal has been waiting at the Berni Inn for an hour and I'm
getting anxious. Arthur's lad, breathless with football, has
swept in and undertaken to make more tea. Arthur is well into
the subject. Randle is clearly a kind of magical charge
illuminating his understanding of most things, as fathers are
supposed to. I am relieved to remind myself that I'm a poet
and not the journalistic hack that might have been expected,
so I stand some chance of being up to the task of honouring
such a potently remembered man.

I separate myself, cautiously and respectfully. Petal, after
knocking back her second double, takes me to a quiet road by
a park where I hit the flask a little until my emotions, curiously

stirred, have properly subsided. There are trees and iron railings.

3

Jim Casey nestles in concrete land with a certain immunity. The BBC building in Manchester is typical in that it is in no way different from any other tower block. There is a smart receptionist, a lift with big smooth buttons, wall-to-wall carpeting, and the perpetual whine of the let-'em-breathe apparatus.

He is an affable, informal man, easy to talk to. There is a strong Liverpudlian twang to his speech. I note this as odd because his father was a Geordie. Meeting these people, I am treading in the shallows of a heady mythology. I am a little abashed by the presence of the son of Jimmy James and I am afraid he might be inhibited by Petal who sits opposite him, looking balefully into the thin air somewhere between them, judiciously banishing any possible hint of a smile as smoky anecdotes are told.

I need not have worried. Casey's ease bespeaks his strength.

He launches into his recollections in short, succinct bursts of language. The secretary works silently and busily while he chats. A colleague comes in and intersperses remarks.

'Randle? Well I worked with him once — only time we worked — er — actually on the same show I was workin' with me father — Jimmy James — and I — I was in his act.'

I ask him if he was ever Eli, that gaunt ghost who haunted the bibulous James with complaints about his rumoured insanity, but no, Eli was always Eli, the tall thin one. 'I was the one with the — uh — funny hat and I was followed actually a few months after I packed in, I went in for writing — I was writing at the time and I decided I was going to write full time.'

'What? Variety scripts?'

'Er — radio scripts. And — er — a few months after me was Roy Castle. . . . But he was a very funny man, Frank. A very funny man, creative man. He was, he became, very vulgar, y'know, all burping and uh — but he was a very very funny man, funny character and — '

Casey is the first colleague I've got to. The Josephs and Blakely were employers, administrators. Delaney was family, albeit unofficially. But Casey is talking like a fellow professional, a comic himself, the son of a genius comedian, and the tales he recalls have the jocularity, the witty intonations, the insight of somebody who knows what twice nightly adds up to.

His stories accord with Delaney's in so far as they are tales of wild abandonment of professional standards, of colossal impudence, arrogance, of endless violence and of great comedy skill. There is no husky concern for the fair truth as there has been earlier in the day with Delaney. And there is something of the focus that comes from the distancing gained by being of a younger generation. The development of things, and Casey's situation in broadcasting, have relieved him of the theatre code that might have inhibited his father.

He recalls the 'Any More For Sailing' sketch. Certain lines — 'A've 'ad nyoomerous offers for this 'ere boat, nyoomerous offers. Wot the 'ell'z t' good of a yoyo t' me?' A moment in one of the movies. Doctor tells anxious father Randle he can go upstairs and see his new quintuplets. Randle bursts into the bedroom. Double-takes between bed and chair and says, 'Oh, you're in bed.'

' — I mean this thing, the "Any More For Sailing". It was the fact that he was alone and obviously. No one had ever been in the boat y'know, the trips, and he was — uh — "Any more for sailing. Last trip before tea. Thu're tekkin' the sea in any minnit." And 'e used to keep the pub goin' by drinkin' beer, and the publican, 'e used to go for rides in the boat and that's 'ow they — er — both lived. Lovely thought.'

Casey can't show me the way to Gus Aubrey, questions, even, whether or not he's alive. We chat desultorily about Delaney's belief that his father was a coal miner, relating the fact to Randle's contempt for professional codes of behaviour. He had always described himself to his secret son as an amateur.

'Y'see, you don't know,' says Casey 'how much of this sort of thing comes through frustration — um — of what happened to you when you were down and, when you get there, my God, you're gonna make 'em pay for it and they're gonna do what you want, y'know, and this happens, not to this extent, but it happens to a lot of people. I think probably he had a monstrous chip on his shoulder from what happened in the early days and uh — ' Casey looks into the coffee that his secretary has tactfully placed in front of him. 'I don't know how,' he says. 'I never heard of Frank being witty — y'know — er — offstage. Like the — they used to talk about Rob Wilton. Everybody used to quote Rob Wilton offstage. I've never heard anybody quote Frank being a witty man — offstage. There was a lot of comedians then who were very jolly — offstage, y'know. They weren't the sortuv like — soul of the party at all — uh — but they tended to be very witty. I mean, Rob Wilton was very sortuv dour, a very dour approach to everything, like my father, but would come out with the most brilliant lines just in — whatever was happening, and I've heard them quote Dave [Morris] and quote my father most of the time but never heard anyone quote Frank. I think — I think he was very subdued offstage. Probably — I mean maybe there was this, this mental problem was partly this, this sortuv introverted thing and that had to burst out — in violence.'

We chat a little more. Jim tells me about the love-rivalry between his father and Dave Morris. About the childhood friendship, about the time they got so deeply involved in busking for the Japanese sailors when they both worked delivering goods to the Teesside docks that they got carried off to sea. Then about the difference between James's comic drunk and Randle's, James teetotal and Randle actually pissed as a rat. The interview is winding up to a natural goodbye. This we effect. Outside the streets are darkening. Petal and I find a pub that was probably quite good before the concrete. We drink five Guinness-and-ports apiece to set the seal on a busy day. The little welt of crimson spreads lusciously out from the centre of the creamy head.

4

The letters are starting to trickle in following the ads. Amongst them is a snappy scribble from a well-practised pro called Ronné Coynes. Enclosed with the letter is a handout for Ronné's forthcoming show at Morecambe. Ronné will be home at Morecambe on Sunday but this is Saturday and it's the last night of *Aladdin* at the Bradford Alhambra. Coynes is Widow Twankey.

I am already planning a trip to the Lancashire coast to visit a number of correspondents, also to plunder the files of the *Blackpool Herald and Gazette*. Maybe it would all be tidier if I left Ronné Coynes till then. The picture on the handout shows a chirpy little man in a Beatles wig and a sharp, braided suit. There is a subtle tact about it as though there is a limit to which a maturing trouper can go in extravagance of style. On the other hand, trip to Morecambe or no, the Alhambra is just down the road and, if the proverb is appropriate, the bird is in hand.

The Alhambra is set in the cement heart of Bradford like a Kunzle cake on a coffin. Its domes and garbled Byzantine style have been newly painted to reassure the public that the Council knows it's there. There have been battles about this musty old laugh-palace. The cement merchants have, so far, recoiled from the display of rampant philistinism which their budget must surely necessitate.

The doorman at the stage door is an art student who recognises me. His cubby-hole reeks of stale beer. The fag ends littering the filthy floor are none too gentle on the nostrils either. Extensive structures of thought concerning the jaunty, tidy style of the showbusiness toper, the lovable pompous spirit of the theatre bar, jewelled pinkies raised from the stem of the gin glass, first and second fingers clenched on a ringed cigar, this set against the sprawling squalor of the young in their concrete Bohemia, form and dissolve as the boy rings Coynes's dressing room.

Coynes's manager, Mr Paddigrew, an ageing Scot with all that special politeness the Scots are good at, comes down to greet me. Yes, Ronné will see me. Scuffling up the stairs of the Alhambra — glimpses of bulb-studded mirrors, whiffs of powder, juveniles tittering under their fairy-doll paint, scattering down the corridor in their tatty tutus like cabbage whites — I marvel that the trail has only now taken me into the gnomic warren of an actual music hall. A scent of it in Leeds when I began, but this is more than a scent. The business is still going on, plain to all the senses. There is to be a Mayor's reception after the show, to mark the end of a long and packed season. Maybe music hall, like jazz, never quite dies.

Coynes is a little man, as his handout promised. He is wrapped in a sumptuous dressing gown. His make-up, still worn from the matinée, ready for the first house, gives him that rich air of benevolent fantasy that is the very marrow of pantomime. Paddigrew introduces us. Coynes's demeanour, like that of any performer happy and proud to be in the theatre, is so rich in mannerisms its falsity is reassuring. An artificiality as genuine as mother's milk. He makes me feel immediately at home. His accent is surprisingly shot through with a strong — Is it Swansea? — inflection. His manager and companion has the politeness of the Scots and Coynes has the natural rhetoric, the narrative skill, of the working-class Welsh.

No sooner, however, has Paddigrew disappeared and Coynes begun to talk than a stagehand, soft-voiced and oddly emotional, pops in to say goodbye and beg a signed picture from Ronné who intends to hit the road straight after second curtain. Ronné has a stack of pics ready. He is a little man of tremendous warmth who loves to be loved, and can easily afford huge measures of affection in return, with all the time-expenditure it entails. Love, I note as the interview progresses, is not too strong a word.

Coynes tells me it was his dubious privilege to steer the drunken and obstreperous Randle from town to town with two touring shows. They followed a disastrous period of confrontation and rupture in Randle's career. One was called 'I'm a Good Boy Now' and the final one, 'Let's Be Frank'.

With Coynes a number of layers falls off this reluctant onion. Like Casey he talks as a colleague but unlike Casey he was an intimate, a kind of nursemaid. Coynes it was who had to get up early on Sunday morning, get around his boarding-house breakfast and zoom down to the local four-star hotel where the star of the show had to be cajoled into the driving seat with no more than two tumblers of Haig and Haig in his skin. Coynes it was who had to turn off his responses of sane alarm as Randle hurtled down those pre-concrete A roads at 80 or 90, groping under the seat for the crate of Guinness which was always there to sustain him all the way to Coventry, Glasgow, Morecambe, Liverpool, Middlesborough, Manchester, Leeds, Blackpool again.

Two of the front-house programme ladies come in to say

their goodbye. They clearly have a very special regard for Coynes. Freddy (Mr Parrot) Davies who is top of the bill pops in. He doesn't command the same response. The ladies get their autographed pictures. Davies recalls Randle, swaps a recollection or two, then disappears to get his face on. Back to the meat of the interview.

The stories Coynes tells are the fag end of the saga. Whereas Delaney had made some point of his father's propriety, his dislike of women swearing (or smoking), his swift apology to his son — 'Forgive me' — when any stagedoor pest had been told to fuck off, Coynes, situated by right of one thing and another somewhat above trite concepts of respectability, gives me the authentic dialogue. The pictures are of a man who would be seen as a sadistic tyrant were he not so obviously a victim. Stories are told that must surely incite some bitterness, some hatred for Randle, but Coynes tells them with affection. The burden of all his tales is that they describe a giant, a man larger than life-size with outsize behaviour, outsize concepts. And of course, a great comedian. A very very funny man.

We are close to the heart of the subject. None the less there is still some secret. Accounts are contradictory as one might expect, pursuing the ghost of a multi-faceted character, but there is a key somewhere and somebody knows it. Gus Aubrey, Coynes tells me, is dead a year or more. Neither he nor anybody can direct me to Queenie or any other girlfriend. Such ladies would in any case have retired long ago, Equity informs me. Fisher's publishers, Michael Joseph, have either lost Queenie's address or don't care to impart it. If a key to the contradictions is to be found it is surely to be found with women.

Outside the football crowds are dispersing, the newsboys are selling the Green 'Un and a host of yattering starlings wheel above the city, gathering along window ledges. Their noise drowns out the traffic. They make the tower blocks look as permanent as sandcastles.

PART III

As You Find Us

1

The comic art of Frank Randle, besides being rude, was also rudimentary. All he did all his working life was to sew embellishments and improvisations around three character sketches that formed the triangular foundation of his work. There was the old boatman of 'Any More for Sailing', the old hiker of 'The Old Hiker', and the subtler, gentler patriarch of 'Grandpa's Birthday'.

He had a tiny repertoire of standard gags that would last a present-day comedian like Bernard Manning about five minutes. They lasted Randle all his life, some of them becoming so familiar they developed the function and identity of a catch-phrase.

The question emerges, then, as to how a man whose verbal repertoire was scarcely more extensive than that of a bingo caller became a hero, not just a good comedian, not just a great comedian, but a king in a primitive sense, a solitary figure embodying the spirit of a whole community.

Blackpool sands. A sweltering afternoon. Family groups sit glued together by a common puddle of cast shadow as though the sweat had rolled down from under those knotted handkerchiefs and cherry-bedecked hats to soak the very sand beneath them. Fragmented bars of 'Chu Chin Chow' drift in from the pier interspersed with the antic splash of the breakers which were savage enough to break your legs at lunchtime. The buskers and hustlers are out in strength. Mr Punch pursues his evil proclivities with a voice like a kazoo. Two men greet their ragtime gal over the chords of a ukulele whose clock-dial drum is as round and dirty as the faces of the minstrels themselves. The five or six pints of ale they imbibed when the tide was high form a sweltering wash of sweat against which their burnt cork is insubstantial. Further down the beach where the sand is wet and firm a group of very drunk miners, still clothed to the neck in fustian and flannel, are throwing big copper pennies on to a tin advertisement for Mazawatee Tea. In its light dusting of sand two 11-year-old boys are swinging their rough-shod feet through a simple shuffle routine. One of them plays 'Lily of Laguna' on comb and paper. One of them is dressed in a grown man's trousers tied at the ankle with string, a huge pair of shoes worn on the wrong feet that rattle and slap on the tin. The inevitable postage-stamp moustache is dotted underneath his nose with burnt cork. His bowler rocks about from one ear to the other. He has a cane which he twirls, bends whips from armpit to armpit, passes across the saggy backside of his trousers. His solo spot is marked by no particular dancing skill, but his deliberate disasters, the unwarranted collapse of one leg, tripping over the cane, catching the falling bowler and re-angling it, are all done with a kind of possessed fervour that earns tremendous response from the colliers. He is, in fact, listening to their responses as closely as he is listening to the rattle and slap of his feet and the peppery phrases of the comb and paper. Each trip and collapse is timed to excite the laughter of the small audience at a time when it is most vulnerable. The boy knows where the ticklish rib is and how to touch it. They know, in their blooded commonality of ale, that, in a most profound way, this funny little boy knows them. His fever is unrelenting, his attack reckless, as though the dance, the sun, the day, the whole situation of beach busking has carried him out of the norms of life. He has forgotten completely that he and his mate, Tommy Hall, have already spent their fare home to Wigan, that he is here in Blackpool to visit his real mother, the gracious and exquisite Rhoda Hughes. He has forgotten the colossal lunch she fed him at Lockhart's Café behind the Tower, where she moves among the tables in her fine uniform like a goddess, and he has forgotten that soon, when the sun goes down in beaten brass over the rising sea, he and Tommy must count their takings and, depending upon the amount, buy a ticket home or buy some sweets and set off on the long night's plod through Preston on down to New Square, Standish Gate. And finally he has forgotten that along the route he will cease to be Arthur Hughes and become Arthur Heath once more. His energy and intensity carry the whole occasion on to a level of experience where a kind of extravagance is accessible. The fervour is manic, mad. The little bugger is capable of anything, so, deliriously and hilariously, anything can happen. His features, popping and slurping in and out of a series of comic-cuts expressions, is never out of communication with the audience. He is never alone, never allows his mind to meander. He has given the situation the whole of his frenetic concentration and has so turned it into a magical situation, something wildly beyond the norm.

Later, having counted their pennies, one-and-six, a bob or two short of a fare, even for one of them, they will bundle up their costumes, throw the tin advertisement into the advancing waves and walk the first leg of their journey. This will take them in the vicinity of Blackpool Gymnasium, and Arthur Hughes, a toffee apple mingling with the remains of his Charlie Chaplin moustache, will be blissfully oblivious to the fact that in a short seven years he'll be tuning his body to a fine level of skill in that male-smelling interior, amongst the sweat-darkened pine and leather, between its echoing gloss-painted walls with its special percussive music of slaps, bangs and grunts. They will pass the Tower where, red-wigged and deliberately inept, in a mere eight years' time he will provide the laughs in Astley's Trapeze act or as one of the Three Ernestos. What he does know, however, is that he is going to a place where men of formidable muscular power and will, tenacious pick-swingers, who, at gala time, giggle while they kick one another's shins for sport, where such men are caught up in a humiliating round of subservience that pounds the very sparkle out of their earnest and ingenious minds.

Arthur Heath has held a very deep respect for the community of working people who have so warmly adopted him ever since the morning when his mother took him from her sister Florrie's house in Kale Lane, New Springs, where he'd been born, and delivered him up Wigan Road, off Standish Gate into New Square and Mama Annie Heath was waiting for him. Here there was a warm old man who could make you laugh and a sister, Lil, who could take care of you. Here there were the people to drench this posthumous child in a security as thick and as warm as mushy peas. This is the house to which young Arthur Heath must walk for the next four hours. This is his home and, in his heart, he is never to leave it.

But it is out of this respect that he has already formed his impulse to withdraw, to circumvent the fatigue, the early senility, the fears and sorry limitations of these kind folk.

On leaving St George's School at 13, then, his stint in a cotton mill was short lived. 'Nathen,' says the foreman, finding the young Heath asleep on the bales, 'th'art tired out lad. Tha'd better get 'ome and get thi some sleep.'

'Aye, an' it'll be a long sleep too,' says little Arthur, ''cos A'm not comin' back.'

At 10, 11, 14, he knew that a super existence was the only existence for him, a long sleep that was, in fact, an incandescent dream of a life, something unknowingly akin to what very different artists were beginning to call surrealism. Nobody was going to quench the sparkle in his mind and he knew he would have to be a kind of superman to prevent them. Firstly, then, he had to get to Blackpool where Rhoda lived. By no means the mother of the floury apron and the woman-smelling body that tucked him up, comforted his tears and smacked his bottom, Rhoda Hughes was, to little Arthur, the Queen of Blackpool, a matriarch of mythic purity and feminine perfection, the fairy on the Christmas tree; and Blackpool, sparkling, bustling, fragile, was the fairyland where his dream existence must be realised.

So to Blackpool he went with growing frequency and, when Rhoda married an ex-soldier called Dick McEvoy who had taken a Blackpool pub, Arthur Hughes and Arthur Heath both became Arthur McEvoy and moved permanently to the coast. Earning a pittance by odd jobs as shop assistant, waiter, bottle washer, tram conductor, he spent most of his time in the

1 'a terrible head' *(p. 17)*

RUBBERFACE RANDLE

A rude noise made him a star

By LAURIE TAYLOR

THE final curtain came down yesterday on slapstick comic Frank Randle's 41 turbulent years on the variety stage.

With his wife Queenie and his mother by his bedside, the "uncrowned King of Blackpool" died at his bungalow home in Bispham - road, Blackpool.

It was goodbye to the famous "Randle's Scandals" . . . a life of back-stage turmoil . . . a colourful character who went down fighting.

Frank was always a fighter. He loved a street-corner scrap in his home-town Wigan as a lad. And there were plenty more fights to come when he took to the stage.

At 15 he got a job as a clown with a tent circus at Blackpool. He graduated to slapstick comedy via an acrobatic team.

And then came success. Big money. And trouble.

His theatrical life was crowded with rows, walk-outs, court cases, and back-stage bust-ups. But he still packed them in. He said: "I'm vulgar, but not filthy."

"as essentially a North - country in.

ne of his films had a national review,

● This was Randle off-stage. But with his teeth out (right) he could twist his face into any shape to suit the characters.

Drunk again

● "Ba-a-a, Ah've supped some ale toneet" —the Randleism that convulsed thousands.

2 'wrought from spiritual elements of the hen run and the madhouse, a strutting, crowing geriatric' (p. 17)

3 'Thu're tekkin' the sea in any minnit' *(p. 38)*

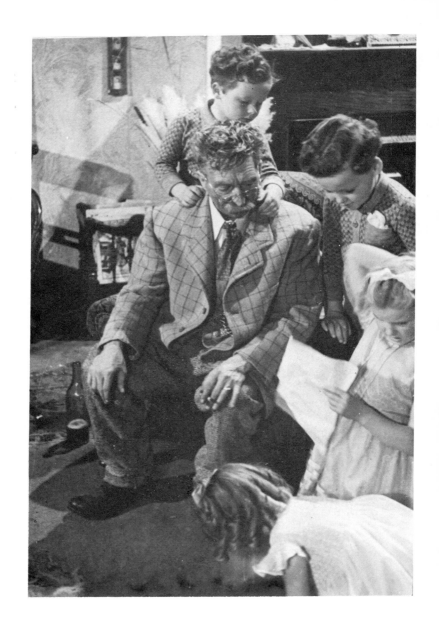

4   'the subtler, gentler patriarch' *(p. 43)*

5 'warm, receptive and, wonder of wonders, she loves him' (p. 49)

6 'a distinguished resident of Blackpool with Queenie' *(p. 81)*

*—and as he was known off
the stage*

Mr. Randle's body will be brought into Holy Family Church, North Shore, tomorrow evening and a Requiem Mass will be held at the church at 10 a m on Wednesday.

FRANK RANDLE
(in character)

7   'his stage personality, far from being a mild amplification of his own offstage personality' *(p. 50)*

8   'disjointed juxtapositions of garments as wild and disorientating as those of Cubist and Surrealist painters' *(p. 51)*

However, as hotly in pursuit of the benevolent forensic image as I was in pursuit of Randle, they did send a constable round to Mr Barnes asking him to ring me. He didn't. That sent me to Directory Enquiries for the seven or eight H. Barnes's listed in Blackpool. Two answered, both the wrong Barnes. Five days later number six answered and said he was indeed my man but there was no point in our communicating because he knew nothing of Randle. I didn't know at the time that Barnes initiated at least three incidents of legal proceedings against Randle for using 'unscripted material'. Neither did I know about the time when he was foolhardy enough to bring Queenie into the argument. I left the thing in suspense. Maybe I'd see him when I got to Blackpool, maybe I wouldn't.

Subversive chums at YTV slipped me a number for Diana Dors after all else had failed. A man told me she had just left to do cabaret in Manchester. John Duncan, who had directed La Dors on BBC TV, agreed to motor me over to Manchester where, in his company, a welcome was assured. On the appropriate morning, however, he rang to say that the cabaret spot had been a one-nighter and the Red Hot Momma of 1977 was back home in Epsom. To the phone again with an ear beginning to look like a Brussels sprout. The familiar whiskey-and-soda tones came rasping down the wires.

She was writing her own memoirs and needed all anecdotes for her own book.

I was ringing at a bad time. She was preparing the evening meal.

When should I ring? Like Barnes, she didn't see much point.

Was I being that much of a nuisance?

Frankly, yes.

Albert Modley, bluntest of the Yorkshire comics, was in the book. His wife, relaying my remarks to Modley, who I imagined sitting in tartan slippers, behind a bottle of Tetley's Special, was reluctant. They had been in an early show with Randle, *Yorkshire Relish*. They remembered the first time he did 'Any More for Sailing' as a front-curtain fill-in; also the postcard he sent signed R. Supparts. They had the records of course. Apart from that they didn't see much point in my calling. Was I in showbusiness myself? "Well, there you are you see. Albert's always hearing from students, universities and such like. He's a bit fed up wi' it."

The letters provided a marked contrast. Whereas the showbiz contacts had been largely professionally defensive, professionally analytic or simply hostile to gentiles who were not of the calling, the letters were coming from a different level. Here were the people who recalled the one time they had brushed against the magic hero and never since got that touch of stardust out of their clothing. Their letters, with their corner-shop notepaper and hesitant Biro longhand, evoked terrace houses, council flats, lonely bedsitters throughout the North.

Two tiny leaves in grey ballpoint on pale-blue lines from Cleveleys:

Dear Sir,
    We read in the Evening Gazette you were asking for information about Frank Randle my auntie had a guest house in Manor Drive Cleveleys and he stayed with her about some 40 years ago.
    My mother lives in Yorkshire she may be able to help you with some information about him if you care to get in touch with her here is her address.
    I hope she will be helpful to you.
        Yours sincerely,
        R. Wales (MRS)

Yellowed newspaper clippings — 'I hope you can make use of them' — from Mrs Roberts of Lytham St Annes.
    Mrs Leah Croft from Sheffield. Blue-lined sheet. Blue ballpoint. Both sides, side two numbered:

Dear Mr Nuttall,
    I was interested in your notice in the "Stage" requiring information regarding Frank Randle the comedian.
    It was in 1928, I was in the same show with a troupe of dancers call the "7 De Reskes". and Frank Randle was the comedian — but he was then known as Arthur Twist as I remember him in the show he used to wear a green felt apron and a bowler hat in one scene. I think he was supposed to be a gardener The show was called "And You" and we rehearsed in a room over a public house in Leeds in 1928. The Company included

Arthur Twist
Harcourt Mills
Annette Williams
Nina Dale
Grace Gordon
Sylvia Moss
Harry Jeanette
Jim Sylvester
Phil Mace
De Reske Girls

Sorry I can't give you any more information about Frank Randle but if any of the De Reske dancers write to you. I would be very pleased if you would forward me their address.

Thank you yours sincerely,
    L. Croft.
Enclosing S.A.E.

None of the other De Reskes ever wrote. Cigarette-carton chic. Back-street Art Deco. A song about a girl called Cigarette. The pub in Leeds was the one where I had prepared to meet the Joseph brothers with two double measures of Johnny Walker.

Maisie Norris of Blackpool had her own notepaper but it was printed some time since — the phone code lettered. The address was in elegant printed script. Her hand, again in blue ballpoint, was ornate and self-assured. So was her style:

Dear Mr Nuttall,

On reading your letter in last week's Stage, I am prompted to reply, giving a little information regarding the early career of Frank Randle, who then worked a double act with a partner on trampoline, as the "Bouncing Randles," in the early 1930's.

My late brother and I were in a review, "Yorkshire Relish", produced and toured round the Northern dates (McNaughton and Moss Empire etc.) by the late comedian, Reg. Bolton; also in the cast was the well-known Yorkshire comedian, Albert Modley, happily still with us and living in Morecambe.

Reg Bolton gave Frank Randle a "front cloth" spot in the

second half of the show, as a comedy single act, in addition to the act with his partner.

This was the famous "Any More For Sailing" routine, in which he worked as a seaside boatman with clay pipe.

This act almost stopped the show at the Yorkshire dates, and Reg Bolton's problem (especially at first houses) was to get Frank Randle to cut his act in order to ring down on time!

I am sure that Albert Modley could give you some items of information. . . .

Marjorie Taylor, from Blackpool, sent pictures of Randle in belted camel jacket and white ducks, with dark suede shoes, binoculars round his neck. Behind him his white convertible and the Central Pier entrance, the very structure into which he was to crash that very car, with a contrasting poster of Randle as the Old Hiker, cock's-comb hair, muffler, *pince-nez*.

Randle, suave in a white tuxedo, smiling up to the North East of the picture, cigarette poised, polka-dot tie with a Windsor knot. 'Happy Days, Frank Randle.' 'To Percy and Marjorie.' On the back of one 'Imperial Repro Studio, 46, Myrtle St., Liverpool.' On the back of the other a list of places indicating a holiday route: 'Neath, Morriston, Pontardulais, Ammansford, Llandyvie, Llandilo. . . .' all the way to Blaenau Festiniog. Happy days indeed.

And a self-caricature of the hiker by Randle, specially for Marjorie. Flash sports-column drawing-style, something else he might have done.

My late husband Percy Taylor. was. his. greatest. friend he. used. to go on fishing. holidays. in. Frank's caravan to Scotland. and went. nearly every week. on Frank's boat. The Namouna which was a converted. life boat so was very sea. worthy. Percy used to moor it off the South Pier and Frank used to sleep on it while he was playing the South Pier show . . . we were probably the last people to see him before he died. His. wife Queenie went back to live near the family and I believe married. again. . . .'

Marjorie Taylor invited me to call. I rang her up and made a date. She was to be my first appointment in Blackpool.

David Godbear, a drummer from Sandowne, Isle of Wight, types on his own printed notepaper — name in blue lettering like they used to have on Kardomah menus. Credentials down one side. The lad is still swinging, has accompanied Dickie Henderson, Pearl Carr and Teddy Johnson, Tommy Trinder, Nat Gonella, Reg Dixon, Roy Hudd amongst others. He recalls Randle neglecting to book a place to stay when *Let's Be Frank* hit Chester Royalty. Pit-drummer Godbear failed to find him digs, none the less came in for special thanks and a last-curtain dressing-room drink. Godbear recalls that the musicians who had to catch the last Liverpool bus left Randle in the middle of his act. Godbear and a couple of violins played a thin version of the finale. Interesting to note that Randle, in his last touring show, a sick man with a long record of violence and disturbance, offset his contempt for management and contract by a most fastidious concern for the anonymous figure, the little man, just as he offset his absenteeism with very frequent double rations. Prepared to give of himself not contractually but in response to authentic impulses of generosity alone.

John Montgomery, a writer and theatre historian, penned a long letter from Brighton — lined foolscap, not letter pad, notebook. Crisp hand. Good fountain pen. Was publicity manager on *When You Come Home*, the only film that Butchers made direct instead of buying from Mancunian — Randle's cinema excursion into sensitive acting — adopted sketch character from 'Grandpa's Birthday' to play adored old man. 'I'm afraid it was *not* a good film, because the script was so muddled,' says Montgomery. 'The director JOHN BAXTER, WAS Absolutely 10st. The film cost twice as much as it should have — six times as much As Any other RANdle film, but I think it mAde less money than Any of them.

'He (Randle) really WASN'T funny in the film; the script crippled him ANd John BAXter WAs such a quiet, charming man that RANdle (who was ACCUstomed to very CRude, rough, tough music hAll treatment And films MAde ON the cheAP) WAS COmpletely out of his element. He blew up ONCE or twice during filming, ANd he WAs ONCe very rude to me, but I gave him plenty back. After which we got ON O.K., especially when I got him a big photo in the Daily MiRROR And other publicity.'

Besides the intriguing correspondence which may or may not exist between Montgomery's erratic sprinkling of capitals and the natural emphases of his polari, Montgomery provides a deal of information. He has photographs which I send off a cheque for. He provides a complete list (with dates) of Randle's movies — something I neglected to ask Blakely for. He sends his love to Nat Jackley who still hasn't replied and he explains in detail what was amiss with *When You Come Home*.

His return letter, with the pics (Randle on set beleaguered by kids — Leslie Sarony's — and starlet — Leslie Osmond), get deeper into the same material. The dialect character comics that didn't translate well in the South, the wide-boy comics who fell flat north of Birmingham. 'None the less his films were shown throughout the South but Usually in small cinemAs — the independents, not the big OdeONS or ABCs or GAUMONTS or GranAdA. However, there were many exceptions, And RANdle's films always did well in WORking clASS districts, simply because his Appeal was entirely to the working clASSES, ANd he MAde NO pretensions to be posh or (as he would say) "La-di-dAh."'

Insight anon:

'I think FR had a chip on his shoulder. He liked good clothes, EXPENsive CARS, And was full of envy when he met people who had what he couldn't buy — education And good tAste. He therefore gained the reputation of being a Very difficult Actor to work with. StAge door keepers have told me how difficult he was — "A real SOd" (I was told at Leeds EMpiRe) — while some people said he was very mean And others said he drAnk too much and threw his money ARound.'

A detailed analysis of why Randle and Gus Aubrey, and indeed the producer John Baxter, were wasted on the poor script of *When You Come Home*. An account of Randle and Queenie at a Hampton Court dinner party, decorous and polite. Useful snippets, the offer of further help. Thanks John.

John Brettargh, ex-manager of the Garrick, Southport. Printed notepaper, address in royal blue Gothic script. 'In variety at the Garrick he went on for George Western of the Western Brothers and appeared in his dressing gown with Kenneth in full tails at the piano. He also got so drunk in the Prince of Wales Hotel that he slept in the smoke-room bar.' Other smoky anecdotes. . . .

And now closely typed sheets from Frank Clarke of Darwen, Lancs. Tight rhetorical paragraphs rattled out of some antidiluvian machine. 'If you're a friend of Frank's then you're a friend of mine, hence the "Dear Jeff" at the start of this epistle. . . . DON'T BOTHER WRITING THE BOOK, JEFF — YOU'VE GOT IT HERE! . . . .'

Frank Clarke was a local photographer and film ham. 'I used to sojourn on the stage of the 'Victoria Theatre,' Burnley, for photography and cinematography — of the chorus girls and dancers of the more delectable delineation. This was early 1940's and I had a round of theatres. . . .'

Randle, after an introductory skirmish about copyright got Clarke into the girls' dressing room with his camera. 'Y'know Frank, those Hollywood cameramen when they're doing a backstage sequence always have shots of the chorus girls doing their quick changes in the dressing room! . . . I stayed till the end of the show — Even after the film ran out. Only a fool runs out of film on such a scene as that!'

Thereafter they were mates. A camera around the neck ('Frank said, "My God, it's better than mine!"') was all Frank Clarke needed to be welcome whene'er his path crossed that of the Scandals.

Clarke includes a poem. 'A Long Belated Tribute. Just As It Came To Me The Day Of Your Letter.'

> You mention his name
> And now we grieve again,
> For one we loved
> In theatres long ago;
> Is such his fame,
> That we retrieve again,
> All that has been,
> All that we used to know?
>
> Still smell the paint?
> And hear the audience murmur?
> The theatre glows
> Before its patron saint;
> As all before in half-expectant fervour
> Seek to recall
> When memory is faint?

So came the Star;
Acclaimed by all before him,
An Actor still: Comedian or not;
Such as you are,
All you who sat before him,
What had he got? — —
He gave his best — that's what! . . .

The lights then dim;
He passes in his glory,
And goes his way,
As we remember him;
Then someone comes,
To tell us all the story;
He lives once more,
We still remember him! . . .

A second letter. Yes, he has film of the Scandals somewhere
in his catacombs. I arrange to call *en route* to Blackpool. He
writes back, welcoming the idea. He includes a short article
about the old music-hall circuits. He has some good points —
'None of these artists needed the use of microphones. The
modern phenomenon of the 'mike-bound' star is essentially of
the present day, as also is the show where little else occurs other
than what can be put into a mike before a black curtain. The
previous age before the limiting influence of electronics
enjoyed fluency of motion and flamboyance of theatrical
vividness and colour — And they *walked* to the theatre usually
staying, as Frank did, in the hotel that was nearest to the
theatre. You could be sure to see them in the street — not
hidden in cars — but walking at your side like ordinary
mortals!'

Geoffrey Lord, an enthusiast from Nelson, sends me
programmes and an invaluable set of cuttings about Sonny
Roy's breakaway group, The Unemployed Scandals. Next
week's attraction, set between K. W. Caunce Footwear
Repairs and Duckworth's Prams on the programme back: 'You
Must Not Touch BUT YOU CAN SEE THE SECRETS of the
NATURE COLONY. THE LATEST FRENCH SENSATION
MODELS IN 3D. Sit back boys — they come out to you — Yes
3D on the stage!'

Cuttings and a sad recollection from Ray Seaton of the *Wolverhampton Express and Star*. Watch-Committee trouble. Alcohol. The early twinges of religious mania — 'embittered and rather plaintive'.

Dorothy Francis rings: 'When I was manageress of the Theatre Royal, Barnsley, Frank Randle gave me one week of hell.' The tales of wreckage, foreseeable by now. 'And his humour — Well, in my opinion. . . .'

Interest, suggestions from Michael Pointon.

A rather manic scribble from John Lovelace of Blackpool — script near horizontal in royal blue Biro. 'Well I worked as Asst. Carpenter Jack Taylor and Frank was second comic Show Shout for Joy year 1935 onward at the *Old* Opera House toured Review also was in sketches.' — A phone call to Mr Lovelace puts him in the Blackpool date book. I have a weird sixth sense that the key to the secret is somewhere with Lovelace.

Sandy Powell's agent gives me a number for him in Eastbourne. His voice over the phone sounds odd — just like Sandy Powell. Yes, he'll try and think up some anecdotes. He writes with rather an odd tale about Randle dressed as a Western gambler on film set (nowt t' do wit' film). I write back asking him about Eva Willis, Arthur Delaney's mother. Arthur had mentioned that Sandy was a main contestant for Genevieve's favours. He replied — a neat typewritten note on pink paper, signed in green ink: 'The Delaney and Lee act. I can only remember they were a good double tap-dancing act, it must be 40 years ago since they appeared on a bill with me.

"Eva Willis was a very pretty young lady, and seemed to be a very nice person, I did not know them very well but they seemed to get plenty of work in those days.'

2

This rash of letters received and digested then. The programme of people to see at Blackpool thick as a workhouse butty. But the years before his joining *Wild Oats* at Accrington are still obscure. Was he really ever a collier. I know a number of colliers very well and have a special regard for them. There is something about the tenor of life dow'n't' pit that makes miners into creatures of extraordinary guts, loyalty and understanding. Can my regard for these friends as powerful spokesmen for the working class (the excitement of the Tories' deposition in 1972 never quite dead in my responses) really overlay into my enthusiasm for certain comedians, Frank Randle particularly, in exactly the same function?

Somebody worked alongside him in the pit or, alternatively, stood alongside him in the betting shop. If he was born in Wigan why did Eva Delaney meet him in Accrington on the other side of the Lancashire coalfield.

I ring Directory Enquiries, the only readily accessible inventory of our fading society, get the names of the papers and put an ad in the *Wigan Observer* and the *Accrington Observer and Advertiser*. The second rash of letters arrive. Again there are shades of the old mill-town environment. Elementary-school penmanship. Village-post-office stationery.

Mrs Purcell of Whelley (Can it be true?), Wigan. 'Frank Randle and myself are cousins. Two sisters children, My Mothers Sister who is the Aunt of Frank Randle she is 93 now, but she will be able to tell you all you want to know' — an address in Skelmersdale, Lancs. — 'if she can't talk so much please go to her Daughters Address which is Mrs Alma Thompson. . . .

'P.S. She is the only Auntie left now.'

A prompt reply from Mrs Alma Thompson corrects my spelling of McEvoy which I had been spelling Mackevoy.

'However,' she says in an articulate and rambling hand, fat loops and squashed letters, 'I have written to his widow asking for her permission to pass on any information as you must appreciate that some of the details are "family skeletons".'

At last. Someone knows the way to Queenie. There the contradictions will be solved, surely, although John Lovelace, Jack Taylor's stage carpenter has given me a curious buzz of expectation. I ring Lovelace. He talks compulsively as though convinced that the inside stories he knows ought to be told. He has been attendant at some witch's kitchen of the past which corruption and hypocrisy have sealed over. Yes, he will see me when I come to Blackpool.

Alma Thompson has given me a number for her son, who will take messages. Daughter-in-law replies. I picture an efficient young wife in a sunlit interior with new furnishings and warm colours. Her mother will be home from work in the local factory about half-five. She will make a point of having her mother near the phone at that time. I ring and make an appointment. It's going to have to be after the whistle blows.

Kenneth B. Bennett from Orrell, Wigan:

'I was a little boy during the war years when he was on the stage at "Wigan Hippodrome" my mother saw him. About two days later the same man knockt at our door. yes what do you want said dad. Do you not know me said Frank my dad stood and thought he said no. And then it came to him. he went to school with him they grew up together at St George school in Wigan and that night and for the next few days they wipe the past years away THAT IS ALL I KNOW.'

Randle was at the height of his money-spinning, grog-swilling fame during the war. Yet, home again in Wigan for a week, he prefers to pass his spare time chatting to his old school friend. The man's elaborate respect for ordinary folk. 'If they're ragged-arsed and merry,' he used to say, 'they're welcome.' Nostalgia for the humble miracles of his back-street childhood. A yearning for anonymity.

J. Thomas of Preston is an adept at copperplate (penmanship — old school timetables, "11 — 11.30 a.m. Penmanship'). In the inevitable shaky ballpoint on the inevitable lined sheets he manages the steep angle, the thin cross-strokes and the broad down-strokes, the Edwardian flourish of a trained and elegant hand.

'You are going back a long while now, and as you say he was a very talented man, he certainly was, and physically a very strong man which probably you didn't know, he was very strong and muscular, that very few people, if any, that have seen him on stage as the "Hiker", would believe. . . .

'He took my cousin Edna "Taylor" in 1937 on the stage, she was then the Cotton Queen, and introduced her to a packed audience that was at a theatre in Oldham and I believe well, I know that it went very much like this — "Ladies and gentlemen, I am taking this opportunity to introduce to you my cousin, a beautiful young woman (18 yrs.) from Oldham this years 'Cotton Queen', Miss Edna Taylor" and I believe she got a resounding ovation. that is going back awhile Jeff. . . .'

Edna Taylor as pleased with this unctuous attention as Kenneth Bennett's father. 'He was the same age as my older brother (now deceased) would be now seventy six had he lived,

my brother often used to take him off in the "Kings Hotel",
Ulverston' (one of the original pubs to which I had written,
whence no response had come — the old mimic already
gone. . . .) 'as they say in Lancashire, to a T. He looked like
him. So do I in features, build and in ways, he once stroked his
nose and said to me, We're alike Jack arn't wi. I said, that's
reet Arthur, but ta's lark our Dick thas getten mure hair on
than me, and mure money, he laughed and said "Well dust a
want ta come ont stage, and I said, I, he replied, aw reet al see
to it, I was about nineteen then, going back a bit further now
Jeff nearly fifty-three years. My memory has faded a bit now
Jeff but I knew him long before that, he was brought up at
429, Warrington Rd, Spring View, Lower Ince, Nr Wigan.
Yours Resp;, J. Thomas.'

Thomas, then, if he has information as accurate as that
address, will know which pit Randle worked down and for how
long; also what was the Accrington connection. I ask him. He
replies. The same sedate and stylish hand — 'Received your
welcome letter, re *Arthur Heath, Arthur McEvoy, Arthur
White, Frank Randle*, the last two being stage names. Expect
that my letter confused you a little likewise will this letter of
confirmation, for instance Arthur Heath, but there you are. I
had wondered where you got the story that he was a collier.
Sure he played at and on pitheads, but he never worked down
or on top of a mine Jeff. My elder brother worked down the pit
my father was a collier, my grandad and his son my uncle were
cage drivers, but Frank Randle never, that part of your letter
made me smile and at the same time brought memories of
sadness some sixty years ago. My brother could have told you
more than I can about him Jeff they played together they were
to us younger ones the 'Big Lads.' and I think they went to the
same school and left school at about the same time at thirteen
years old. Yes! I think he knew George Formby after he left
school but not before, George lived in Wigan, we at Spring
View which is only about ten minutes sharp walking away, and
so my brother told me and shown to me where in Wigan the
three of them went to work on leaving school, I am not sure
now but I think that my brother worked in a grocer's shop
'Frank' in a chemists and George in a shop there as well and
that is how he must have got to know him, but as I say I am

not sure, but he most certainly to my knowledge didn't know him before then.'

The letter flows mistily on. Randle's physical strength is again underlined, his prowess as a boxer. A trampoline act called the Bouncing Dillons is recalled. Jack Thomas himself can still snap a six-inch nail with his hands. He can not, however, despite the muscular prowess, understand Randle's later violence. Nor does he recall the Accrington show *Wild Oats*. All he remembers is that young Frank used to busk Blackpool beach and often had to walk all the way home to Wigan having spent his fare. One sentence, however, stands out — 'I don't think anyone could write a biography about Frank, Jeff, and if we do meet sometime I will explain what I mean.' The key? Somewhere near it. I write again asking what does he mean. The reply is obscure. Un-named people know un-named things. . . .

A wild enthusiastic scribble from Shevington, near Wigan:

'My husband and Arthur as Tom knew him were great little pals and I am sure they would both be pleased for me to pass on to you the things they used to do as children together.

'I myself have had many hours listening to the antics they got up too.

'In fact I have lots of things no one else knows of they had no money but lots of happy times out of dressing up and dancing their funny little dances. I even know where they got their hats and dresses.

'I have often wished it could be written of it would have made a good story if I can help at all I shall be pleased to do so too their memory. Yours Mrs Florence Hall, Tommy Hall's widow.'

The letters dwindle. A letter from a second cousin recalling that McEvoy senior was a soldier, that the Randle career began at Wigan Little Theatre, recalling the fact that all relatives, however remote, were always made welcome in the dressing room. Mrs Fielding of Blackburn whose husband had occupied the same hospital bed as Randle and wrote to say so with all good wishes, and then got a letter back — meticulous attention to the anonymous people.

Finally from Derek Andrews of Chorlton-cum-Hardy, panto recollections and a batch of photocopied programmes from

Hulme Hippodrome and Blackpool Central Pier, including one for Cinderella. Round the panels where Potter and Carole promise 'FUN ON MOTHER'S SETEE' and Evie and Joe Slack promise their 'CHEF SPECIAL', G. Thorburn offers to solve 'Your Racing Problems', A. E. Benn's Temperance Bar offers 'Home Brewed Herbal Drinks and Hesta', while a Specialist In Ladies and Children's Wear, offers 'Tasteful Clothes at Prices To Suit Everyone, Coats, Dresses, Blouses, Skirts, Knitwear and Underwear'. Andrews says, 'I have seen many fine performances in over thirty years of theatregoing and my favourite performances are as follows, Wolfit's Lear, Olivier's Othello and Frank Randle's Buttons, it was indeed a brilliant piece of theatre.'

It's clear that the little people got nothing from Randle but starlight, belly laughs and close, respectful attention. The scabrous tales of outrage are relayed by colleagues and employers alone, despite their professional reluctance to do so. Randle told Delaney he was an amateur. It certainly becomes clear that for most professionals he had a deep-seated sense of alienation.

PART V

A Merry Old Soul

1

Queenie's king behaved like one. He swept into the lifestyle, the fame, the licence of a monarch with mediaeval ease. The voices in his head had indicated his destiny. The subsequent facts of his career merely bodied forth his own version of himself as a super-human. The possibility of his ever sinking down a pit, or foundering in a cotton mill, disappeared by right of a certain deeply struck bargain: 'I will embody you and represent you, just as long as I don't have to do the fucking work.'

To the end of his career he never lost his fear of the pit, of the mill, of an ignominious finish 'selling rubber ducks on the Golden Mile'.

There was an interim period after Reg Bolton thrust him in front of the curtain with nothing more than a memory of a Blackpool boatman. Nevertheless, during this time another memory, that of a wildly chauvinistic old man he'd met on the Manchester to Blackpool walk in 1922, served as a basis for the hiker sketch, and the memory of Grandpa Hughes, Rhoda's dad, and Grandpa Heath, both served to inspire Grandpa's Birthday, a sketch which always ended with the arrival of Grandpa's father to top the celebrations. Rough and extrovert

Auntie Janet from Scholes lent a good deal of her kitchen raconteur's panache to all his stage characterisations. Once there he had struck another shared area. Every family has its grandpa but every community, until the planners and social workers moved in, had its collective ancestor figure in the Village Idiot. Village Idiots, besides being the red-nosed comic prototypes of the comic postcards, or the gormless lads of the Dougie Wakefield, Our Eli, kind of image, were wild old labourers, split from family and regular employment. Touched with psychosis and sodden with alcohol they were likely to be found in the outbuildings of the town, a barn, a cowshed, a derelict quarry, an open-cast pit. As grandpa was the affectionately held scapegoat of the parlour so the Village Idiot, Jack o' Nowt, Jack o' Judy, Owd Tom, could be blamed for all unsolved crime, even murder, could be persecuted and pilloried for awhile and ultimately, always, forgiven. Thus the community could forgive itself for its own neglect. Children played with the Village Idiot, both as playmate and, if he be dead drunk, as toy. He was likely to expose himself from time to time, stagger drunk down the main street unimpeded, pass a saucy and perceptive remark to spinsters and widows along the route, and was invariably held to be secretly rich, to hold property in a neighbouring parish, have a biscuit tin of big white fivers somewhere underneath the disgusting pile of rags on which he slept. He was a rural figure who carried on into the life patterns of the small cotton towns like clog-dancing and pace-egging. To the industrial community he embodied a certain degree of bucolic nostalgia. He was up to his shanks in shit like a farmworker, so involved in the natural life that he had no more need of hygiene than the beasts of the field. Bernard Miles's comment on his own dirt — 'When that gets thick enough that'll fall off same as it do off a tater' — corresponds to the old Hiker's pert reply to Dr Scollops about his filthy feet: 'A'm a damn sight older ner thee.'

Thus he had the goat's fabled fertility. A common figure for the community, food and milk was put out for him as they are for the fairies. He was immune to law and guilty of all sins. He was the Holy Fool, the naïve shaman. He was also the original comedian. That Randle saw this, saw the connection with his home-parlour prototypes and made it yet another means to a quite extraordinary fame and privilege, guaranteed that his

art was on a different footing from that of the other more
skilled music-hall stars.

The Village Idiot is a synthesis of his community and Randle
was the synthesis of the industrial North. He absorbed and
caricatured to a monumental degree the qualities of the class
and the place. The North was simple. He was a broad to a
degree. The North was vigorous and optimistic. He was a
sportsman and an athlete. The North was direct and deflatory.
Randle was, as the *Manchester Guardian* put it, the 'master
of the single entendre', besides his deeper earthiness as a visually
orientated artist.

Chasing around Wigan in his adolescence Randle had
known another funny little shop-assistant, the son of a
well-loved comedian, who was to embody the North in a
different way. Randle's synthesis turned a face to the South
that was not merely defiant — it was aggressive. George
Formby on the other hand, was apologetic, flattering, boyishly
charming. Randle profoundly needed to enter the South and
take over like the stars of a Cup Final. It was never to happen.
Formby, whose character was as innocent and engagingly
feeble as his stage role, slid into West End success almost by
accident with *Zip Goes a Million.*

But when Jack Taylor whisked the young Randle off the
trampoline forever in 1935 he coupled him with Formby at the
Blackpool Opera House in *Shout for Joy.*

The show, a great success considering the fact that two
comparatively unknown comics were being launched, was
awkward to tour with. The lavish spectacle, in best
Opera-House tradition, was so difficult to mount the curtains
went up fifty minutes late at the Stratford Empire in London's
East End. Formby, whose wife Beryl ran all his affairs, who
struck a very hard bargain, was left behind. Randle was the
comic and *Shout for Joy* toured the entire Moss Empire Circuit
from Stratford to Glasgow and back. In Glasgow Randle, a
hard competitor who saw most things in terms of mutual
power, recoiled from the city's reputation for violence. A
working-class hero with a supernatural awareness of collective
consciousness in the North of England, he felt himself stranded
before the austere sardonic mood of the Glasgow tenement
dwellers. The Gorbals was a long way from Oswaldtwistle. The
warmth was going out from the old boatman and nothing was

coming back. Every night he made for the wings to find a stagehand posted there by Jack Taylor to send him back into the limelight. He clawed for the bottom of the backdrop but stagehands were ready for him and stamped on his fingers. Finally he fell into the orchestra pit. It was an early manifestation of a strong and peculiar trait in Randle's professional identity as he saw himself. 'Not a professional — an amateur. . . .' So the nature of the operation was not sore duty nor hard necessity. It was a caper, a lark. Something Randle and his pack of mates got up to, like a game played by a mob of ill-shod urchins round Wigan market. The hard terms of contract were something to be taken with a tip and a wink.

The following year, after *Aladdin* at Sheffield, when he found himself alongside his childhood pal Formby once again, at the Opera House, the starlight into which both talented scamps were ascending was clouded by Randle's aggressive competitiveness and his wild disregard for contract. A BBC team under Barney Colehan come to broadcast the highlights of the Blackpool season got Formby but left before Randle's entrance by rising stage. The following night Randle came slowly up as directed, properly attired for his performance. 'Ladies and gentlemen, it's perfectly clear that George Formby is the only star of importance in this show, so George Formby can entertain you now,' he said, and walked off. Formby himself was stuck in a faulty lift. Improvisatory powers were stretched but Randle didn't give a damn. He already had himself cast in the public role in which stunts like that were entirely acceptable. It underlines his claim to that role that the Lancashire audience were ready to grant him his crown and the Lancashire management was compelled to acquiesce.

Taylor's *This Is the Show that Jack Built* made a bid for the West End. The West End touched Randle's interior paradox with swift and cruel accuracy. He was out of his kingdom and, in many ways, out of his depth. The *savoir faire* of the West End review was entirely opposite to his style. None the less, his Queenie was a Londoner and, in so far as she embodied the mother who dumped him, she seemed to him to demand the London success that was otherwise irrelevant for a king already more than halfway to his throne. Further, London entailed a betrayal of the real mother, Mama Heath, and the earthy back-alley solidarity which she represented, the solidarity that was his access to sovereignty. When Sir Oswald Stone criticised the show's lack of polish, a quality that endeared it to the unpolished North, Randle vented his rage on the unfortunate extra with whom he was performing a boxing sketch and knocked him out of the ring clean into the stalls.

On With the Show on the North Pier the following summer saw him further into the seat of privilege. He was by now a distinguished resident of Blackpool with Queenie enshrined in a big posh house, first on Devonshire Road, a new house, then on Forest Gate, a huge house, then 'Westwood' on Whitegate Drive, eventually Craig Royston, on the Lytham Road. He was an inevitable in each summer season, oscillating between the piers, the Queen's and the Opera House, whilst his own road-show, Randle's Scandals, toured the cotton towns. He comforted his audience by showing them that he understood and shared their state. They were in no doubt that he was of their sort. Besides all his other attributes they could tell he was their sort by his knowledge of the conformities to be observed, and beyond even that by the kind of snotty buggers who walked out. Thus he relieved them of those conformities, lifting them out of the double standards their communities were built on.

2

Human behaviour springing from collective identity is either moving and noble or it is vicious and degrading. In the working class it springs from a clear knowledge of shared vulnerabilities, physical, biological, economic, psychological. One suffers from fatigue, from silicosis, from angina and all the other afflictions endemic to industry and heavy labour. One suffers sex, both its frustrations and its abuse, the over-proliferation of children, the guilt, the puritan disgust. Engaged on manual work one's body decays early. Any vanity or sense of physical beauty dies early and is subsequently detested. And there is the perpetual penny-pinching need with its side-effects of domestic need and sore envy. One is cheated, then, of many pleasures and one is largely cheated of knowledge. One hasn't the words to argue one's case. One is perpetually terrified of betraying oneself and one's class by betraying ignorance. A community that knows it shares all these qualities is a community enjoying a sense of common spirit which is expressed in compassion, a rigid fairness in the sharing of scant means, a warm suspension of privacy and status-seeking. Mama Heath, Spring View, New Square, his mate Tommy Hall, Jack Thomas and his brother, any relative or old pal who presented himself at the dressing-room door, represented all these things for Randle. Late in his career when the scandals hit Wigan the star would slip round to Jack Thomas's terrace house, stick his feet on the mantelpiece while Mrs Thomas was getting the supper, saying, '*This* is what I call home, Jack.'

Besides kindness, however, community breeds taboo and aggression. It is forbidden to seek ostentatious individuality. Exhibitionism is forbidden. High style is suspect. Articulacy is to be checked unless it be in the community service, hence the arch language of trade-union officials. Sensuality is distrusted as a quality that should be kept on a level with food and drink — functional, incidentally pleasurable. And in some tight communities anyone pretentious enough to get up and leave will be so broodingly envied he will never be forgiven.

Randle's familiarity with these anxieties allowed him to play with the tensions they engendered, building them up, teasing them and then releasing them in explosions of laughter.

As for the significantly alienated, throughout his Scotch-sodden reign he was pilloried by the early leavers who wrote to the press, by the Watch Committee, and by the police. Harry Barnes, the new Chief of Police who took over in the mid-forties, was a particularly rigorous crusader against the cavalcade of events his predecessor Holmes had allowed. Making maximum use of the byelaws remaining from the 1880s when Blackpool was still trying to preserve some vestiges of its original respectability, bye laws by which the only entertainment allowed on Sundays was Indian Pavilion material, musical and formally dressed, Barnes exercised his anachronistic Methodism. Vic Oliver found himself in trouble for using the 'spoken word' on a Sunday at the Hippodrome. Randle, fed up with Sunday restrictions, sent Al Read on in his place but the laconic straight face raconteur flopped instantly. On the 17 June 1943, Randle failed to appear in *This is the*

Show that Jack Built at the South Pier Pavilion, having seen
the letter the management had just received from Barnes.
Complaints had been received, the Chief Constable claimed,
from members of the magisterial bench (the Watch Committee had, in fact, been called off the golf course for
emergency discussions). The complaint was concerning
'unsavoury matter' and 'business'. Randle stomped out after
expressing himself to Barnes direct, and Norman Evans was
called in as a replacement.

More difficulty followed in August 1946. Police officers
visiting *Tinker Taylor*, again at South Pier Pavilion, brought
evidence that the agreed script had been embellished with
gestures which were 'disgusting, grossly vulgar, suggestive and
obscene'. The sketches under attack were 'Grandpa's Birthday'
(with Gus arriving as the Grandpa's old flame), 'The Prodigal
Son', and 'At the Bar', in which Randle and Billy Pardoe
played a couple of lads on the batter taking the piss out of a
pansy, pansy played by Aubrey. A lot of play with a back-view
nude painted on the backdrop was the root of most of the
offence. Aubrey said in court that he could scarcely be accused
of using unscripted material because he'd never seen a script.
Randle rejoined that he hadn't yet received his summons and
would they please send him one as quickly as possible. There
was much talk about the difference between what may be
considered offensive at the seaside as opposed to what is
offensive nearer the hearth. Finally Randle was fined thirty
pounds, Pardoe and Gus a fiver each, and Taylor one pound.

Much of the time Randle was able to deal with these
situations before they came to court. Two Manchester
plainclothes men warned Randle that a certain line must come
out or there would be trouble. Randle went on, reached the
point where the line was to follow, and then turned away from
Cinders to face the audience: 'Ladies and gentlemen, I am
now supposed to say, "Hello Cinders, I've come to cut off your
water" but the buggers won't let me.' Later, when the officers
presented themselves at the dressing room, Randle said, 'Now
then, we're all grown-up people here. I did what I did, I said
what I said. Either come in and have a drink or piss off out of
my sight.' Well, it had been a hard night, and the whiskey was
an exceptionally good brand.

In September 1952 two more representatives of the law

attended Randle's Summer Scandals at Central Pier. Without Taylor, under his own auspices, at the hub of his own empire, Randle had been going more than usually wild all season. There was the parson who swore like a navvy, pulled a lady parishioner's skirt down when it 'rode up' as she sat down to play the harp: 'A see yi've got 'em on again.' Who addressed his congregation with, 'What a collection.' There was Aubrey queening about in tight Boy Scout shorts ('a homosexual impression' counsel stated) producing knitting when Randle stroked his arm. And there was the Cinders sketch with the 'water off' joke and exchanges like — Cinders: 'I want to talk to you.' Buttons: 'It's nowt t' do wi' me. It'll be me father again'; like Buttons, being offered Cinder's favours: 'A'd rayther 'ave a boiled egg'; like Buttons making much of groping Aubrey's massive tits: 'Ah, falsies! A'll buy thee a better pair tomorrow.' There was objection about the silent Chinaman who shuffled across the stage: 'Is that King Farouk?' And finally there was Randle in exceptionally baggy trousers gurgling: 'And if all that business 'ad been submitted to the Lord Chamberlain it probably would never 'ave been allowed.'

Other items of offence were, 'There's a flea loose in the harem and the favourite will 'ave to be scratched' and 'There was a young man named Vickers who took his girl to the flickers. He saw some wool and started to pull — A nearly med a bloomer there.'

Randle was fined ten pounds on each of four summonses, Sonny Roy and Gus two pounds each on each of four, and John Capstack, theatre manager, was fined two pounds on each of two summonses.

It was at the end of an outstandingly disruptive season that Randle appeared front-curtain after the finale, immaculate in tie and tails, gold *pince-nez*, his best set of teeth in.

'Ladies and gentlemen, you have seen that the little show we have presented for you this season has been under a great deal of criticism. You have seen that certain citizens, some of them quite eminent, have seen fit to call our performance "filthy," "obscene", "offensive" and that may well be their opinion but I come to you, ladies and gentlemen, and ask you to be my final judges. I am, like you, a simple man born of simple folk, a man of the industrial North of England. My pleasures are simple — my packet of Woodbines, my glass of Guinness, the simple joys of the seasons. Simple people of our kind understand the facts of life in a way that many of our critics do not. You will know that my little bits of fun are founded upon the facts of life and, because you understand life and the realities of life, I ask you to be my judges.'

Moving down into the audience now, amidst cries of 'Tek n' bloody gorm on 'em Frank' — 'tell 'em t' bugger off owd lad' — taking stretched hands, touching shoulders. 'Is my little show obscene?' Thunderous no. 'Is our little entertainment disgusting?' 'Tell 'em t' get stuffed, Frank.'

Back up on to centre stage. 'Thank you — ' with a catch in his voice. 'Thank you ladies and gentlemen, for your comfort and encouragement.'

Backstage, standing on the good side of a stiff Scotch he asked Buddy Burgess, 'How d'you think it went?'

'Fine, Frank, fine,' said Burgess, scarcely able to believe his ears.

'It was from the heart, Buddy,' he said, 'every word of it.'

3

The obverse side of the coin whereby men long for the security of belonging to a community is the secret longing of each individual to escape its restrictions, the geographical restriction of the locale, the cultural restriction of the class and the moral restriction of the community; in the case of industrial communities to escape the puritanical superstitions of Methodism which still waxed strong in Randle's time.

In these days of efficient contraception when sexual repression is almost completely vanished amongst younger people, it is difficult to imagine the explosions of hilarity and shock that could be released by a word that sounded like tit, a word that enjoyed a remote assonance with fuck or cunt. Thus Frankie Howerd praised his 'Mrs Farquhar' and Randle larded his impromptu patter with similar devices. 'Friar's Balsam to you!' The *double entendres* that he shovelled into his cameo scripts were appealing not despite but because of their infantile simplicity. Verbal subtlety is a main weapon against working people. If there must be words at all, let them be simple.

Girl: 'Excuse me, but could you tell me the way to Oldham?'
Randle: 'You know lass, if you ask silly questions you're
    liable to get silly answers, but if you sit down and let
    me have one with you I'll go one better.'
Girl: 'How do you mean, you'll go one better?'
Randle: 'Well, I won't tell you the way, I'll show you. . . .
    Do you like a man's company?'
Girl: 'Yes, especially if he owns it. . . . Don't you think that
    necking is like wrestling on TV?'
Randle: 'No, I don't know as I'd say that.'
Girl: 'Wouldn't you?'
Randle: 'No. In wrestling some of the best holds are barred.'
Girl: 'Have you had a family?'
Randle: 'When I was in my pomp the wife gave birth to
    three sets of triplets on the trot.'
Girl: 'Did she?'
Randle: 'She did and I got the King's Pardon. . . . I'll
    always remember, the parish council laid a taxi on to
    fetch the wife from hospital. . . .'
Girl: 'And what happened to you?'
Randle: 'They kept me in hospital under observation.'
Girl: 'Whatever for?'
Randle: 'They wanted to know how I did it. . . .'
Girl: 'Isn't marriage funny? A girl walks up the aisle with
    one man and down with another.'
Randle: 'And a man marries one woman and has to live
    with another.'
Girl: 'Do you mean a girl changes after she gets married?'
Randle: 'No, I was thinking that she usually brings her
    mother to live with them.'
Girl: 'Are you illiterate.'
Randle: 'No, my mother and father were married.'
Girl: 'You've kept pretty fit haven't you?'
Randle: 'I put it down to miniature baths.'
Girl: 'Miniature baths?'
Randle: 'Aye, one minute you're in and the next minute
    you're out. . . . Two chaps called round the other day
    about some little interference. I thought they were from
    the tellyhire at first.'
Girl: 'And weren't they?'

Randle: 'No, they were from CID. They'd come about my
  youngest grandchild, our Egbert.'
Girl: 'What had he been doing?'
Randle: 'Having carnival knowledge of a girl . . . (*belches*).
  Manners. . . .'
Girl: (*picking up newspaper*) 'It says here that Khrushchev
  has diarrhoea.'
Randle: 'And God bless the girl that gave it to him. . . .'

The wedding sketch with Aubrey — when Randle, with a
gurgled 'Shall we get to the point?', shot his hand straight up
Aubrey's skirt — had such dynamic impact in the days when
women could be arrested for wearing a sun-top, that Randle's
reckless use of such material underlines his faith in the licence
which his rock-hard solidarity with his audience gave him.
Whilst always remaining one of them, he had realised their
wildest dreams of escape to such an ostentatious extent that he
transcended the usual brooding hatred such an escape
engenders, earned mirth and further adoration because he
had demonstrated that escape was actually possible. He was a
man who could say owt and get away with it.

This, then, in the forties, was Randle arrived at total
privilege. Having failed his medical for the RAF, pacified his
conscience with a spot of Home Guard duty, with his summer
seasons, his travelling show Randle's Scandals and finally with
his films, he was the roaring regent of the Lancashire coast.
Gunning his Lagonda, his Bentley sports model, his MG down
Lytham Road at 80, crate of Guinness under the seat, Paisley
choker adrift in a breeze that could take himself and his
(always) male companions to any one of a dozen little pubs, or
else to the Circle Bar at the Queen's, or else the pierhead bars,
he could wind up, a pile of rolling garrulousness, at the
Farmer's Arms. And after the show, unless something formal
was arranged at Craig Royston, maybe to his yacht *Namouna*,
moored conveniently at the end of South Pier, or his handsome
touring caravan bought so that Queenie could accompany him
in film work, parked not too far along the Bispham Road.

His manner was shot through with a number of alternate
moods. He could ring the changes on all his offstage
characters. If one should get overly drunk, why then he could
become the other and start again, and if all were drunk he

could hand over to his erstwhile chauffeur Horace from Wigan who would pull up outisde the Farmer's just in time for the Governor to fall out on the kerb like a sack of rather expensive rags. If, late at night, his car swooped into that terrible zigzag, he would hoot his super klaxon, and if that failed, if a tram, stationary and unmanned, refused to move, why he would slam straight into it as he once slammed straight into Central Pier box office. And if the magistrates asked him why, he would tell them. He'd sounded his horn. It hadn't moved. What could he do? The magistrate's court was, in any case, a second theatre to Randle. Here he was the actor, the advocate, the engaging rhetorician. Here, if cross-questioned about his 'unscripted material', he could slip with ease into a re-enactment that would have the entire courtroom purple with suppressed laughter, then leap back on to his high platform of legal argument. In 1952 alone he had no less than three drunken driving charges. And in '53 defended himself with the following version of what must have been, in any case, an hilarious *mêlée*: 'My offside wing struck this vehicle a glancing blow and scraped alongside its full length. Then I immediately applied my brakes full on. Again I felt a sudden kick to the right. The car stopped. I felt around myself to see if I had been hurt. I then tried to open my driving door. It would not work. I turned down my driving window and shortly afterwards a figure appeared which I recognised as one of the Blackpool Constabulary. I said "Good morning officer," and he replied, "Oh hello, Frank. Are you all right?" I replied, when my voice was drowned by a babble outside the car. I was asked to get out of the car but I could not as the door appeared to be jammed. I asked the officer to help release me. Another figure approached, the door was prised open and I got out. It was dark. The officer receded a few yards and said, "Walk towards me." A torch was flashed in my eyes. I approached the torch. The officer said, when I reached him, "All right, Frank." I heard another voice which said, "This man has been drinking." I asked the man who he was and he said he was the driver of the vehicle. I told the man to leave the matter to myself and the policeman. The man was shouting and there was a bit of hysteria in his voice. I began to realise that this could be serious so I asked the driver if he would repeat, "The Leith police dismisseth us — Truly rural, rurally regular —

and Good morning said Eve to Adam, good morning sir, said she." The man got slightly annoyed and said, "I will punch you in the fucking stomach." I replied, "Sir, I don't like your attitude. I don't like your choice of words. I don't like your threats, therefore, I must remonstrate with you, and furthermore, I object to being punched in the stomach." I then took hold of the man's coat and drew my hand across his throat in case he carried out his threat, telling him I would not let go unless he apologised. An arm came between us and I was pushed back by an officer who said, "Don't start that fucking game here." I had to support myself by placing my hands on the officer's arm. I offered to drive the officer to the police station. I was later taken to the police station where I was introduced to Dr O'Riordan who seemed a nice sort of chap. I said, "Good morning, doctor," and held out my hand which was ignored. I must admit at this juncture I got a little annoyed. I was escorted through a grill to the first room on the left where I undertook some tests. It is true I twirled round in the middle of the office but it was a ballet movement which showed precision, timing and co-ordination.' The ballet routine had, in fact, stood him in good stead on previous occasions when it rendered the arresting officers too helpless with laughter to carry out their duties.

He lived the life of a Munchausen, joined the Bispham hunt and fell off the horse at the first canter, appeared, none the less, in hunting pink for dinner with Joseph Locke and his wife at Craig Royston. On such occasions he was the grand actor. An invisible astrakhan collar was about his neck, an imaginary sombrero on his head, a silver-knobbed cane near visible in his hand.

Yachting apparel was much to his liking as, occasionally, was a highland chief's regalia. He anticipated the rock 'n' roll stars of twenty years hence with the get-up of a Western gambler. Two pet dogs, Fifi and Patsy, floundered in his wake. One Queenie's, the other a waif from the pound. Symbolic.

With Locke, the stentorian Irish tenor to whom love descended like a nangellah twice nightly, and Percy Taylor who ran the local taxi-fleet, he formed a diabolic liaison. Locke, a capable man with the bottle and an eager man with his fists, was a familiar figure among the race-track professors and the bill-shuffling brotherhood of the Fylde half-world.

Together he and Randle resolved that their way of life had nothing to do with income tax. It was part Wigan guttersnipe and part regent that went down to the office after second house on Saturday night and collected anything between a hundred pounds and a thousand pounds in 'readies'. With Locke he was the libertine drunk, the tap-room roarer, whilst for the Blakelys he could be quietly spoken, even timid, and for friends and family he could be the nicest bloke in the world.

It was with Locke that he conducted his most direct foray against the managerial class, the promoters and entrepreneurs, and the South. Because even though Queenie and her ma might want it, as they wanted him to become Roman Catholic, and even though he himself might want it as he glimpsed those levels of gentility which Rhoda had always symbolised, he knew that he could never join whole-heartedly the sophisticates of the South. It would cost him a crown he already had and the endless tolerance that went with it. Out of the mill he may be, and not just forgiven but loved for it. But he must keep it quite clear to those who struggled behind in the soot and the grime that he hadn't joined the other side, the gaffers and the toffee noses.

4

Currently, English society possibly more prosperous and egalitarian than it's ever been is skewered, like a supermarket chicken, on the profound hatred the working class holds for anybody not sharing its condition. The farther away from London you get, the simpler and broader the issue becomes. It is more than a resentment about the class slavery of the nineteenth century, about under-privilege and ignorance and humiliation. It is more than a desire for equality and freedom and enlightenment. It is in England, a desire for revenge, a savage wish for counter humiliation.

So Randle's transgressions went further than his transgression of the taboos of the cotton community. He was naïvely concerned to transgress the taboos of society as a whole, in its organisational layers. He was compelled to tear to ribbons those very barriers of hypocrisy and pretence whereby the classes differentiate their identificatory modes of behaviour.

The five per cent of the audience that arose and left tut-tutted and wrote to the local paper about his splatherings and belchings. Off they went, scuttling up the aisle with their netted hats and their brown shoes, living proof that Randle in his fame and wealth was just as rejected as the back-to-back labourers were, and by exactly the same people. Privately Randle, the idiot monarch, had his own class confrontations.

By the mid-forties there was a lot of money to be made out of Frank Randle and Lancashire showbusiness knew it.

Besides his producer, Jack Taylor, who was, much of the time, a friend, and the huge national network of Moss Empires where artists cut their teeth, there were the Blacks, George and Alf, at the Opera House, and there was Jimmy Brennan who owned the Blackpool Queen's and Hulme Hippodrome among a number of other theatres. It was Brennan and Randle who, with Joe Gummersal, Fred Emery, Harry Moorhouse, had found the Parsonage, Manchester, converted it into a film studio and sold it to Blakely. Brennan was adept at the fast and profitable sale. He was also adept at booking artists at minimum rate because he was quite simply so powerful that a Brennan contract couldn't be refused. 'You and I,' he would characteristically say, 'don't measure our friendship in coinage of the realm.'

Randle, at pains to maintain his fidelity to the people he knew and liked, the 'ragged arsed and merry', was always keen to demonstrate his independence of the Taylors, the Blacks, the Brennans and the Blakelys. There were times when his true loyalty, his loyalty to his subjects, was best served by spending the night the host and the guest of all in the bar across the road from the theatre. And there were the times when Randle, the 'amateur', the Wigan alley lad, would re-affirm his grasp on his fundamental identity by skiving off for days at a time, leaving film sets idle and touring companies wildly improvising, while he and Jo Locke roistered round the cool tap-'oiles of some undetectable Pennine hostelry, or else, alone, he zapped his currently unbuckled sports model up to Cumberland where he would spend days with a comfortable level of ale in him, throwing crisps to chickens over some lichen-covered five-bar gate. Wherever he was, however, to the

Blacks, the Brennans and the Blakelys it was Randle gone again, something you had to put up with, the original sin to be encompassed if you wanted to skim the cream of that particular pecuniary pudding called Frank Randle. Only Radley and Co. of Queens Park Hippodrome, Manchester, took proceedings. They got their three hundred pounds damages but sacrificed the thousands they would have collected had they continued to employ him.

It may have been a resentment of Formby lingering from the *King Fun* days. Nevertheless, whether Formby as guest of honour was the cause or not, large quantities of booze turned Randle and Locke, the old firm of iconoclasts, into a couple of whirling dynamos who, in turn, transformed Jimmy Brennan's Lytham hotel, the site of the celebration, into a Mack Sennett set. Despite the caviare dribbling down the regency-stripe wallpaper, icy smiles were accomplished and hush-hush gestures to press and police, were immediately effective.

Barred for a season from the Opera House in 1951 (Randle chalks F. Stooge says, 'It's a K.' Randle: 'Why is it every time I write F you see K?' Curtain.) Randle bombarded the city with toilet rolls from an aeroplane and presented himself at the stage door every evening for work should the decision be reversed.

On another occasion, following a packed week at Hulme Hippodrome, a group of family and friends were gathered round in the star's dressing room for drinks and congratulations. Randle liked his dressing room. Stocked with a crate or two of Guinness and a bottle of the hard stuff for chasers, he made it a combination of boudoir, salon, office and public bar for the week wherever he went. Arriving at the Garrick, Southport, and being told that the star's dressing room was not available he proclaimed: 'No star dressing room? No fucking star!' and betook himself to the Bold Hotel where he slid comfortably into a week's worth of booze. But at Hulme things had gone well, each house over-running by at least an hour, that great laughter-balloon nodding gently and perpetually against the ceiling of the auditorium.

'Cut it down on first house Frank. The folks ont' second house 'ave got to get 'ome.'

'Gerra bloody ticket!' exclaimed Randle, knowing that flying to Mars was, if anything, easier.

And now close friends were gathered for a quiet drink while the echoes of a riotous week blew away over the Wirral to the Irish Sea. A short knock introduced manager Powell with a piece of paper which he thrust under Randle's nose beside the whiskey glass. 'It's yer bar bill, Frank. They want yi to settle up now.'

The temperature distinctly changed. One of the connotations of a successful week was hours of inane generosity spent in the theatre bar. Laughter was owed to the public. Loyalty was owed to the public and, beyond that, they and the nameless little men who made the theatre's wheels turn were welcome to a bottle of beer, even a bottle of Scotch, and hours of informal company. But Brennan Enterprises, now that was a different thing. Brennan, Randle's one-time partner, had just made a fat bankroll out of Randle's talents and the people's labour. When Brennan's asking hand showed, the impulse of kingly generosity was apt to dry up, whatever the moral reality of the situation. Which way would the adrenalin flow this evening? The face relaxed from its sequence of joy-boy masks and set into the muscular, forceful, even grimly cheated, face of a tap-room hard-case. 'This isn't mine,' he said. The mood had run cold, cards come up spades. The conviviality blew away over the Irish Sea along with the audience laughter.

'It is yours, Frank. Yi must pay.'

'That is not my bill. One hundred and thirty pounds? I've not drunk that much. I'm not mad. Take it away.'

Powell at the door. Randle pacing about. He takes out his gold cigarette case and flicks a Woodbine into his mouth that, best teeth in, has grown set, humourless under the sharp little spiv's moustache he powders out for his performance. The family and friends stand round switching their eyes from carpet to ceiling. Taking small, self-conscious sips from their glasses. Queenie, beautiful, even austere, looks as though nothing is happening. She might be a woman waiting on a station or sitting in a café, something fatalistic about the aura surrounding her.

'I can't tell 'im that,' says Powell. 'Pay the bill, eh? And then sort it out wi' Jimmy later. . . .'

Randle strides from sink to radiator and looks out of the window into the dim street below. He draws at his cigarette like an invalid at anaesthetic. The smoke mingles with clouds of condensation on the window pane. Queenie adjusts an errant lock of hair in the dressing-room mirror.

Finally he is back at the dressing table. He opens his cheque book, rips his swingeing signature across the cheque, hands cheque and bill to Powell. Then he clears the whiskey from his glass and hurls the glass into the dressing-room mirror. His face, set even harder now into some form of undersea rock, light gone from his eyes. Nothing left but the cold and purposeful enactment of profound rage. Walking past Powell he takes the axe from the firepoint in the corridor. He cracks it down on the sink. A swing at the row of wardrobe hooks brings the whole fitting hanging adrift into the room, splattering plaster. It sticks outward crazily like a fractured limb. The carpet torn loose from the lino, tacks like dragons' teeth along the edges, is calico in his hands. The velvet curtains likewise.

He stops and looks round like a craftsman surveying a finished job. That done, he takes his cashmere overcoat which Queenie smooths on to his shoulders, takes his silver-knobbed stick and turns to Powell. "Well,' he says. 'I'll be going then, Mr Powell. It's been a good week. When are we back again?'

'October, Frank. Nice t' see yi. Cheerio.' A warm handshake. Queenie is ushered out to the waiting car.

Dressing rooms shattered like fairy-tale mirrors. The slightest spark could drive the light from those wild eyes so that the muscle in the head swelled and predominated like a visor and everything in sight registered brooding, tearing wrath.

Jimmy James, arriving at a Lancashire hall in the early fifties had to take No. 2 dressing room because No. 1 was shattered. Randle had been there the previous week. At the Theatre Royal, Barnsley, having set the stage for a boxing ring which he never used, having had the doors re-hung because he couldn't stand the squeak, Randle did for the dressing room with a rage like a sledge hammer.

But certain managements were immune. 'We never had any trouble with him. He was always all right with us.'

Early in the forties Randle relieved himself of the cut-purse punters by forming the Scandals. In all of its ten thousand spectacular transformations, the Scandals circulated the seamy old music halls of the North and, occasionally, the rougher areas of the South, for ten to fifteen years.

JIMMY CLITHEROE

Ernie's

cottageful of

memories...

...OF JIMMY CLITHEROE
AND 'RANDLE'S SCANDALS'

From left : **DAN YOUNG**, **FRANK RANDLE** and **ERNIE**

BLACKO TOWER, plonked solidly on a dome-shaped hill near Nelson, seems a far cry from the parade ground — or the stage. But in a picturesque cottage in its shade lives tall, broad-shouldered **Ernie Dale**, first man ever to thrill an audience with that rollicking tune, "The Sergeant Major's on Parade."

9 'his gang of lunatic urchins' (p. 56)

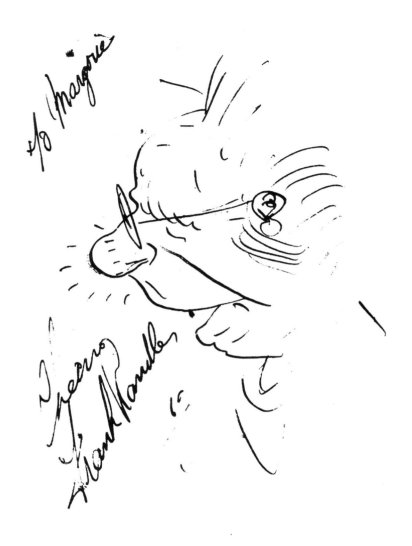

10   'something else he might have done' *(p. 66)*

11 'the script crippled him' (p. 67)

12 'profoundly needed to enter the South and take over like the stars of a Cup Final' *(p. 79)*

13 'could ring the changes on all his offstage characters' *(p. 87)*

Gus Aubrey

14 'drenched in the wistful pathos of the philosophical harridan of misfortune' *(p. 95)*

FRANK RANDLE

PHILIP KELLY

GUS AUBREY

SALLY SUMMERS and DIZZI

SONNY ROY

15 'demonstrating that you could run a theatre company more or less along the lines of a street gang' *(p. 97)*

OVERTURE—The Palace Orchestra will play
popular melodies—M.D. James White

1 **MEET THE SCANDALS**
Entire Company will introduce themselves

2 **NEWSPAPERS**
News in Brief

3 **JEAN CHADWICK**
A-la Gracie Fields

4 **ON THE BALL**
Football Gone Mad

5 **FLORENCE WHITELEY'S FAMOUS**
" ZIO ANGELS "

6 **KAY SOTHERN**
A Smile and a Song

7 **GUS AUBREY**
The "Lady" they all talk about

8 **KENTUCKY**
Entire Company bring you memories old and new

INTERVAL—" The Pirates of Penzance " by A. Sullivan
Played by the Palace Orchestra—M.D. James White

16 'and now that you have all flown from the edge of the nes[...]
be too inclement' *(p. 129)*

District Telegrams : "BESTERMS"

ciety, Ltd. 13 Cannon St.
Preston

_OYED

A L S

AL	9	**RIDING ON A RAINBOW** Entire Company
liances r RVICE REET	10	**JACKIE HERRICK AND SONNY ROY** Boy meets Girl
	11	**ARTHUR CANNON** Maestro of the Banjo
	12	**THE PETERS BROS.** Variety's Mother and Son
Y N	13	**ERNIE DALE AND BOB HULME** Brilliant Entertainers in their latest successes
	14	**SONNY ROY** The Funny Boy will make you all laugh
E . 2619	15	**FLORENCE WHITELEY'S FAMOUS** " ZIO ANGELS "
	16	**SIDE BY SIDE** Entire Company will say Goodnight

GOD SAVE THE QUEEN

Programme Subject to Alteration

Company Manager .... BRAD ARNOTT
Choreography .... KAY SOTHERN
For The Unemployed Scandals
Extra comedy material by Sonny Roy. Gus Aubrey's gowns
designed and executed by Arthur Forster of Darlington.

All Children must be paid for.
Responsibility is disclaimed for the unavoidable absence of any
Artiste announced to appear.

that the storms you may weather may not

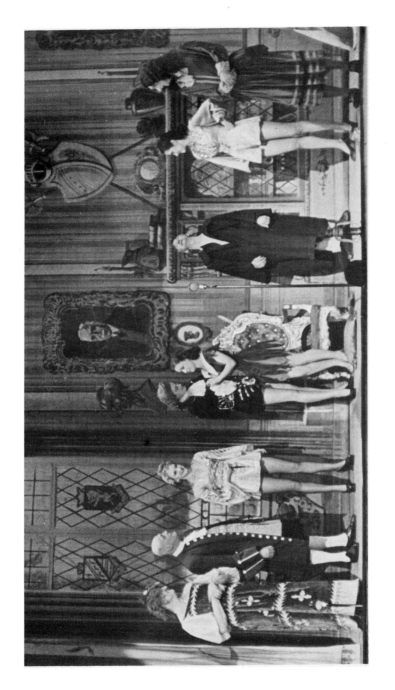

17 'Cinderella draws out better music from a monkey-skull with a barrel-organ mind' (*p. 122*)

The shape of the show was pantomime. There was always a story-line in case anyone needed one. Constant factors were the Mandalay Singers, compromising just about everyone in the company, including an Arab acrobatic act. Their quality oscillated between weighty patriotism, with a hard core of good singers, and total knockabout, miming *Messiah* to a record. Such sweetmeats were included as Florence Whiteley with the Zio Angels, Sally Summers and Dizzi, Hal Mack and the Dancing Demons, Hal Swain and the Swing Sisters, Irene Mansel, Don Carlos, Raymond Waller and Joseph McGovern, Rita Shearer at the Hammond Organ, the Kerry Pipers Band with dancers, Stan Stafford the Silver Voiced Navvy, the Ben Abdrahlman Wozzan Troup and good old Gus Aubrey heading the list of that changeable gang of stooges and enjoying his own solo spot in drag as a seaside landlady or a vamp.

It wouldn't be an exaggeration to describe Aubrey's relationship to Randle as that of a jester to the king, although, in this case, both were jesters. Whilst Randle was a man's man with both feet well in the working-class neighbourhood soil regarding sexual roles, Gus was a drag artist, effeminate, sensitive and homosexual, at a time when the theatre was the only place where the taboo, indeed the law, against homosexuals, could ever be eased in the least. The music-hall drag act was a curious comedy area of perverse self-deprecation. Therefore to the whiskey-swilling gym-trained Randle Aubrey was simultaneously a kind of comic favourite, an object of sadistic contempt, a mild embarrassment and a paternal responsibility. Gus's stage personality was drenched in the wistful pathos of the philosophical harridan of misfortune to whom each terrible blow of fate is no more than a woman of experience might reasonably expect. Randle it was, who, with Joe Locke alongside, closed a failing panto at Oldham Empire and crashed unceremoniously into the Hulme Hippodrome panto where Gus was, for once, the star. Randle it was who persuaded Aubrey to follow his example and have all his teeth out, 'or yi'll never be a true artist, owd lad', and the very next week sacked him. In fact, at times , Aubrey's rate of exit and entrance from the Scandals was as fast as the proverbial fitter's elbow.

Family group in Randle's dressing room. The star is wiping off his make-up with the customary glass at his elbow. Message comes from Gus. 'Mr Aubrey wonders if you could lend him a few bottles of Guinness, Mr Randle. He's got some people in.'

'What the bloody 'ell d'yi think these are? Pit props?'

Similar family group. Gus, sacked earlier in the week, shows his face to say hello to Queenie. So devoid of grievance, so charming and gentle is Gus that the visitors are beginning to feel angry about Randle's adamant silence. His whole attention is riveted on the dressing-room mirror where he is twisting his face into a series of unbelievably malevolent knots as he swabs off the Number Nine. All Gus's remarks, whether addressed to Randle or not, are pointedly ignored. Eventually Gus says his goodbye.

'Cheerio, Frank.'

No reply, and then, when the tall, fragile man's footsteps have almost receded —

'Gus!'

'What?'

'Ten o'clock Monday morning. Crewe.'

'Okay, Frank.'

Randle ruled the Scandals with a rod of vulcanised latex. People worked for a pittance out of adoration for the bibulous tyrant. They had to be prepared to be summoned on stage to sing the Hallelujah Chorus and do physical training halfway through the show while the Guvnor sat on a hard chair and conducted with a beer flagon. An acrobatic act upstaging and neglecting one of its members could find itself unceremoniously sacked and the victim promoted, while the star himself enlivened life offstage by challenging wrongdoers to lethal drinking bouts and otherwise doing as he bloodywell pleased. The compensation was that, besides working with the king, the king would support them in difficulty to a most extraordinary degree. Having placed Pat Williams, the aged stooge with the cup of water for the dressing-room fire, in a Brinsworth Home, he then, at the old man's plea, whisked him out and levered him into the cast of *When You Come Home* in his old comic role as Grandpa's Dad, and then, later, when the old lad died without friends or relatives, Randle lashed out generously for funeral expenses.

With the Scandals the star was his own boss and everyone else's. Divinely free of all but the most punctilious theatre managements, demonstrating that you could run a theatre company more or less along the lines of a street gang.

Meanwhile he was turning every (admittedly slight) effort of Johnny Blakely ever to be a respectable film director to hilarious ruin with his cry of, 'Can A mek it up now, Dada?' His *contretemps* with Diana Dors ended in a trip to Lytham Airport where Randle and the blonde bombshell hired a plane and circled over the Fylde for an hour or two with nothing more to trouble them than a couple of bottles of Haig and Haig and the inevitable crate of Guinness. What Diana Dors represented at that time was West End glamour, an uninhibited, sexually liberated beauty demonstrating Metropolitan freedom from the class strictures on which Randle's sovereignty rested, also her espousal of the rootless American mode. Her revelations, made a year or so later, concerning her husband's jolly games and her participation in them, demonstrated an imaginative and guilt-free sexuality that the British had always previously driven back into the sea. Randle was applauded in his fracture of taboo because he paradoxically never deserted the class whose restrictions he had broken. Diana Dors had never suffered such restrictions, however. In Randle's view and in the view of Randle's subjects she hadn't paid her dues. Whatever innocuous social exchanges took place as the plane circled over Lytham Airport Randle was demonstrating a symbolic capture. Free and swinging Dors may be, but when confronted with Randle the sovereign figure, she was symbolic booty. Nowt but a tart.

Working with Diana Decker in Butchers' *When You Come Home* he wasn't exactly able to make the same gesture but he did create a furore when she upstaged him in the pages of the *Daily Mirror*, bombarding the publicity manager, John Montgomery, with a shower of back-street Wigan and getting a shower of back-street Port Said right back from the recently demobbed Montgomery.

Queenie was a correct demonstration of femininity. Chief Constable Harry Barnes, confronting an already aggressive Randle who thought he was being victimised, suffered a full explosion of Randle's volcanic violence when he tentatively enquired if Randle would like his wife to hear his scatological material.

And ultimately, beyond the Brennans and the Blakelys, beyond the starlets and Outraged of Bispham, there was the South, a place not to be joined as, he considered, Gracie Fields and Formby had joined, but to be conquered, and the capital of the South was the West End.

The early experience with Sir Oswald Stone who stopped *This is the House that Jack Built* for its lack of finesse set the tune and nobody ever played a different one. Although the East End audience lapped up the stew he served he could never refine the subtleties or play down the gastric base of his humour. To have done so would have changed the whole nature of what he was doing. There are people who are happy to be reminded of their common physicality — 'the facts of life'. There are those who are uneasy. And there are those to whom such reminders are positively painful unless tempered with the wince of mortality which is the mark of the sophisticate.

In 1952 Jack Hylton, the distinguished bandleader turned entrepreneur, decided yet again to direct towards the South some of the profit that was pouring into the pockets of the Brennans and the Blakely. None the less, the extraordinary show at the Adelphi into which Randle was supposed to insert short mimes — the sewing-on-a-sleeve-button was the starter — between sets of the BBC programme *What's My Line?* was an early flop in which the distaste of the London critics was helped along considerably by the death of George VI. Randle, having exhorted near-empty houses to move down to the front rows, displayed his surviving brisk optimism by raking together an emergency team of the Scandals and opening at the Met where he played successfully to the working class as usual. Short years later his last metropolitan engagement finished in early closure as he staggered around the stage of the Chelsea Empire too slewed to command even his bedrock skills of gesture and timing.

That these engagements laid bare the king's fundamental hostilities is indicated by the occasion when Hylton and a number of the starch-fronted representatives of 'the London end' entertained Randle to dinner at one of Manchester's most resplendent hotels. The crumbs of the last course were long ago swept away. The brandy had been served while a long-suffering waiter of a great age hovered tirelessly around the flanks of these tireless indulgents. It had long been Randle's ploy to pass out Woodbines, his favourite brand, to anyone whose charisma seemed to demand it. On this occasion, refusing the fine cigar he had been offered, the star thumbed an old Capstan tobacco-tin from his waistcoat pocket and picked selectively amongst an assortment of dog-ends. Having singled out the best, not one less than a whole inch in length, he offered the tin round the table reclining into his comedian's intonation: 'Would you care to try one of these?'

All, of course, declined, so the star turned his attention to the waiter. 'What about you, laddie? Would you care for a smoke?'

'A wouldn't mind, Frank,' said the waiter, the late hour indicating a permissible suspension of formalities. Swiftly Randle's hand moved to his other waistcoat pocket. The tobacco tin disappeared and a solid gold cigarette case was flourished open. The old man enjoyed an oval-moulded Abdullah while the star drew staunchly on his docker.

With his own folk, then, the star could do no wrong. Of all the people who were sacked, short-changed, bullied, abused, few bore him anything but profound loyalty and affection and this was not just because he balanced his tantrums with great generosity and kindness. Kings, for the short span of their appointment, are afforded divine rights. In return Randle made sure his transgressions advertised his loyalties.

This was never more clearly seen than on the occasion of a mayor's banquet following a particularly stormy year in a stormy career.

The gesture is conciliatory. A new company has been formed and a new show is going on at the Queen's. The company, many of them new to the tenor of life with the star, are waiting apprehensively with the mayor and mayoress for the star to arrive before all move into the banqueting chamber to dissolve past ill-will. There is a brisk breeze on the sea front. The company reassure one another with tight little grins and palmed cigarettes. Will he turn up in his fishing gear? Will he fall out of the passenger seat of a chauffeur-driven car waving a hip flask and blaspheming mightily?

His car appears along the broad road, zooms closer, overtaking three vehicles in one swoop and boils to a halt outside the chambers. Randle is crisply attired in white ducks, blazer, Connemara golfing cap and choker. The mayor steps forward to greet him. 'Mr Randle, may I say how honoured I am to extend a heartfelt welcome to you, our most distinguished citizen.'

People are relaxing now. The smiles become real. He is sober and collected. There will be no scene.

'Thank you, Mr Mayor. However, I must insist the pleasure is mine entirely. It is an honour indeed for a troup of humble players to enjoy the full panoply of civic hospitality. Shall we move into the banqueting chamber?'

'One moment, Mr Randle. This is my wife.'

'Well that's your fucking fault owd pal.'

PART VI

The Sort of Thing They Don't Tell Yi

1

Petal's jalopy is not at all well. Despite a series of well-meaning lads who press their hands to their grease-smudged hearts and assure me that they have put all serious wrongs right some other wrong emerges and the scurrilous little vehicle stalls somewhere throwing lives into danger and spurting adrenalin down the adrenalin-prone systems of myself and the owner. An expensive overhaul and a new battery would seem to be some security towards a week's banging about around Blackpool.

We set off mid-day Sunday, stutter up on to the motorway, then, the engine having cut out, bowl back down again coming to rest on Elland Road just outside Leeds United football ground. There we meditate upon concrete for two hours of a concrete-coloured afternoon until the mechanic climbs out of his Sunday pint and breathes hesitant life back into the banger. Waiting, we have long opportunity to marvel how eleven belligerent lads who know little more than how to kick a ball around can ever cope with the landslide of displaced identity in which they are currently half-buried. All those feckless, super-energised Welfare State kids whose house would have been distinguishable from all other houses by style of doorstep, curtains, and front garden ten years ago, whose street would have been distinguishable and whose city would have possessed its own architecture, its own face, ten years since — all those kids scooping up the community identity — no place left by which to locate it, impossible to identify with a concrete block exactly the same as a concrete block in Gloucester, Southend or Hamburg — unloading that community sense on a football team, and unloading with it all the savage neuroses loss of security would seem to provoke. Elland Road, once a ritual arena in the heart of Hunslett, the abominable slum which Richard Hoggart described with such love and warmth in *The Uses of Literacy*, is now a terrifying Nazi monument — Buchenwald floodlights at the corners, turnstile to keep the mutually murderous kids away from one another with their bread knives and steel toe-caps. It is surrounded by concrete — industrial estates, high-rise flats, red brick with the surface and colour that indicates that it is a mere brick façade on a heart of solid cement. M62, M1 and their tangle of slip-roads, underpasses and catwalks, are overhead. The jalopy, reignited, growls up on to the M62 with an enthusiasm I have come to distrust. Through unbelievable mists of roaring road-spray we climb over that familiar stretch. Today the drizzle is so thick we can't see the mill towns dying on either side.

Not until we turn off towards Darwen anyway. There the weather clears. Between Bolton and Blackburn the moors bear travelling blades of sunlight and the little towns sprawl in Sunday afternoon torpor. Each time we stop for traffic lights you can almost certainly hear someone snoring behind the nearest window pane. Two old ladies waiting at a bus shelter direct us to Frank Clarke's. We are two hours late and I am apprehensive. Friends looking at Frank Clarke's letters have warned me that he may be more intrusive than helpful. None the less, the promise of film footage compels me.

We park up the hill from the tiny blackstone terrace house and knock on his door. He is short and thick-set with a shock of white hair. His lower lip hangs a little, ready for the formation of Lancashire vowels. His clothes hang loosely about him with a reassuring shabbiness. He wears his galluses over his grey woollen pullover. Daylight has long been banished from the room into which he shows us. An Art Deco sofa enjoys its senility before a primitive but effective electric fire. The wire elements curl like piccaninny's ringlets, glowing and fading fitfully. Behind the sofa a table. In front of the window a small cinema screen. Before that, radios, TV, video monitors. Opposite, dominating the whole interior like some sinister sacred idol, a cinema projector of the kind that stuttered to a halt in the middle of many a flickering Saturday-morning cowboy serial. A huge, black, blunt-snouted deity with one drum directly above the other and all its plumbing showing.

Frank expresses sympathy about the car, says: 'Sounds like the condenser' and asks us would we like a cup of coffee or something. Tea we say. Coffee he says. He only drinks coffee so coffee it'll have to be. He busies himself off into the back of the house and clatters things, chatting back through the open doorway. He has a number of questions he wants to ask and has listed them with things he must be sure to mention.

Petal wants to powder her nose. 'It's through thur,' he says. 'Works toilet, yi know. . . .' Whilst she's locked away with her needs he tells me that one of the first things Randle asked him was did he make any, could he get any, under-arm films. He doesn't tell me what the answer was.

Coffee served, Nescafé in a diversity of mugs, he asks his questions and goes over the stories in his letters, bestowing on them the immediacy of his enthusiasm and a good deal more detail. He has a Lancashire accent as thick as dripping, consonants formed against the back of his teeth rather than the roof of his mouth, 't's consequently attracting a fugitive h. When did his friendship with Randle begin? 'About um — It would be in the 1940s — the — er — um — because I'd got my — The war would be on — when I met 'im — because I'd got this wonderful camera which was a Paillard Bolex with triple lens, turret and everything. They're still great machines, Bolex machines' — Far from being intrusive or dominating, Frank is cheery, effusive and chatty, an ingenious old lad who extends his hand to a number of talents and interests and wants to talk about them. As other people's lives might be measured and punctuated by the possession of houses, guns, cars, wives, Frank Clarke's is punctuated by the possession of various pieces of cinematographic equipment.

He makes the point that never in all the years of knowing Randle — well enough to be invited to meet Queenie at Craig

Royston — he never felt he could or should be acceptable unless he had his camera with him. An odd talisman of identity. Better, though, than a football team. He and Randle connived to get past stage managers and film certain stunts — 'A went on and A said — "Oh," A said, "A'm from British Paramount News and we must 'ave a picture right away" — and A'd me coat on and belt on and trilby 'at and A — A was somethin' like a newsreel man, the way A was dressed — '

He recalls various sketches and punch lines, the style of the man, and also his prowess as an actor. This is significant in the case of Randle, who did more than amplify his offstage personality. Clarke's memory in all this has been assisted by hypnotic disciplines. 'To bring Gus's name back to mind A did in — A tuke — ah — A tuke — A tried for a week and couldn't think of the name — so A did the auto-hypnosis method wi' the counting system an' it came up in two seconds when A'd done it that way, fetched it up in two seconds, the name Gus Aubr — From nowhur, from the subconscious y'know — wi' — wi' the hypnosis.'

To Frank Clarke Randle and Formby were not just great entertainers. They were 'vurry prone to be met in the sthreet'. He saw no violence, no unpleasantness. Like royalty they presented well-nigh faultless examples of civil behaviour. As with royalty, their excesses were colossal and private (Randle's anyway), their public face most of the time impeccable. 'Yes — 'e was quite — er — 'e wasn't swelled 'eaded and wasn't conceited. He was approachable. He was — er — a friendly man — 'e was very friendly and 'e was pleasant — Not at all conceited. Not at all given to showin' off offstage. A was told 'e did too much to help other people. He never seemed at all downhearted. If he was at all downhearted he was concealing it successfully from me. He was genial. He was fluent. He was flamboyant. He was expressive.'

Frank finds a bit of film with variety material on it — he thinks a juvenile dance act. He hasn't had time to search out specific Randle material. He loans me the reel and we make our way back to the van. It putt-putts merrily along the road through Preston. Outside Preston, on the slip-road to the Fylde motorway, it stops.

2

Petal and I aided by a sturdily built WPC, push the jalopy into the shelter of the overpass. We book into a terrifying Bed-and-Breakfast where the bedrooms are furnished in raspberry jelly and a Scottish psychopath in dirty jeans is in charge of reception. Escaped to a pub called the Withy Tree (Lancashire is wooded with them) we noticed that the Lancashire personality seeks ridicule, is happy to be laughed at. The bar is devoid of that dangerous belligerence which lies as heavy as wet sacking on a Yorkshire pub. A little man leaps around, pop-eyed, quite complimented by Petal's hysterical yelps. At breakfast the only other guest laments about cornflakes under his plate, is suffering from lack of sleep because of the — '*Ooo* it *woz* excitin' — 'E fur murdered t'job lot' — late-night movie.

Yet another lying mechanic empties my pockets and we roar on to Blackpool.

The *Gazette and Herald* librarian, shy and pretty, shows me to a long, brown, scissor-scarred table in a long, brown room. Under the tittering eyes of four silly girls engaged on God knows what distortion of factual reportage, Petal and I proceed to sort a pile of yellow and dangerously fragile news clippings. The giggling girls are too much for Petal. She flees.

I sift and note as many headlines as I can, then ask the librarian to procure for me sorted and dated photocopies. I note two names, one a man who wants to start a Randle memorial society (copy dated '73) and the other, William Burgess, the author of a strong and informative article. The angel lady with all the facts gives me addresses for both and tells me William Burgess, a well-known character who everybody calls Buddy, can usually be found in varying levels of sensory alacrity at the Farmer's Arms.

I leave, phone Joseph Locke — no answer — and a hotel which has let our accommodation go. Petal is snoozing away the lunchtime (five pints and couple of brandies en route across the Fylde) across two seats of the van. We go to the Farmer's Arms. Buddy Burgess isn't there but his address is just around the corner. Leaving Petal reflective over a therapeutic three-star Martel I find the address. A dishevelled Latin who shows me up to the dark landing tells me to knock hard. Burgess responds to a pounding that threatens the very joists. Grey hair, brushed flat but for one or two errant strands. A flimsy dressing gown that has served its master many a tea-stained winter is clutched about a man who, like Petal, is surfacing from his after-lunch repose with some difficulty. The odours of impecunious retirement seep out of the room around his silhouette.

'A bad time, squire. Who are you? Who? What? Randle? My God. Oh my God. Good God. Randle? Well I'll be. . . . Very bad time. How did you find me? Farmer's Arms?' (Crafty little smile.) 'How did you know? Some other time. Yes. Frank Randle, my God. Oh boy oh boy oh boy. *What* a character! *What* a comedian! The Farmer's Arms. Tomorrow lunchtime. Eleven. Okay, twelve then. Very bad time, squire. Tomorrow at twelve.'

On to Lytham. Ring Locke again. No luck, no Locke. Profitless searching for him up and down the hotel bars along the St Anne's sea front. We have a terrible Italian meal and stay in a terrible hotel. Nobody is in attendance in the Residents' Bar. The whiskey bottles with optics and glasses are on a revolving rack on the bar. I help myself and in a strange fit of honesty tell the late-arriving barman and pay him. The hotel is full of noisy middle-aged traders on some very badly organised conference. Later Petal tells me that, descending at three in search of anti-dehydrative orange squash, she finds them rolling around the ground floor like turds in a bedpan.

3

Marjorie Taylor lives in a triangular house. There is a turret, a well-kept garden, a lot of red-brick ornamentation and a wrought-iron garden gate that doesn't feel as though it gets opened very often.

'How's that for timing?' I say with a rather perilous jocularity.

She is a neat, smart woman with freshly set hair. She shows me into her sitting room where the furniture, once well-worn, now looks as though it will never be worn out. She is steady, confident, and a shade resigned. Were I Marjorie Taylor (gothic thought) the ticking of the wall-clock would have driven me stark raving gaga by now. She looks as though she would have no difficulty in marrying again but she moves as though she doesn't give a damn whether she does or not.

Her husband, whose absence is so strong in the room, met Randle through a common interest in boats, cars and engines. Percy Taylor serviced the yacht/houseboat that Randle kept on the end of South Pier. They were boozing mates, Percy and Frank, and that's the way it was for years.

Even though he had a big house in Whitegate Drive Randle had his own separate world in a number of country boozers where he went with Percy. 'He used to go fishing — We — er — went up to Scotland fishing, Percy did. He — was very fond of 'im really. . . .

'Well y'see he changed so when he — when he met. . . .' She balks a little and I reassure her by saying that a certain warm permissiveness in relationships has always been one of the characteristics of showbusiness. So she continues, describing a catastrophic change in Randle's character and giving the reasons for it. Because he used to come here and he used to say, "Come on, let's go" to the so-and-so and have a drink. And he wouldn't let me. He used to say, "Let's go to the Saddle and — those small pubs, y'know" — and Percy used to say, y'know "What about Marjorie?" and 'e used to say, "Oh we're goin' where there are no women. We — er — go in the pub and we drink us pints. We don't want women."'

She moves over to the bureau to look for a Brighton address. Was anyone incumbent in the boat whilst Queenie was in the house? 'Oh no, no,' says Marjorie. 'Nobody ever lived with 'im — or anythin' at all, in fact.' I wonder flickeringly how much anything these libertines didn't do. Maybe quite a lot of anything never happened in those days. . . .

It becomes clear that she had known other friends better than Queenie in those days — 'He wouldn't let anybody go to the house or speak to Queenie or — she had a miserable life really — Never went out unless his mother went with her. We never went much to the house. He was even jealous of Percy calling if he wasn't there — this real streak that spoilt it, spoilt his own life really, spoilt it all really. . . .'

She returns to her chair with a bundle of papers. 'He came here one day and he said, "Oh I must go," he said, and Percy said, "Oh you've only just come. Warraya want to go for in a morning?" So he said, "Well — er — I'm not so sure of the window cleaner. . . ."'

She tells me some grim stories about some tortured relationships and says she wouldn't want them to go in the book. And then, like all friends, she seems anxious about presenting an over-negative picture. 'And yet he was very good with 'is own cast y'know. I used to say, "I wish you wouldn't 'ave that old man with the cup of water y'know—putting the fire out — in that Grandpa's Birthday sketch" — I used to say, "Oh I wish to goodness, I wish yi'd — " and he used to say, "Well I can't sack 'im. I'll give 'im something to do." But he was — um — as funny offstage as he was on really. You know, he would speak on any subject an' — only thing was, he would have made more money if he'd stayed as a comic instead of wanting to produce, y'know — and dress up in evening dress' — My mind shuttled back to Clarke's remark — 'and — um — be the director instead of going on with his humourous sketches. Towards the end that's more what he wanted to do, y'know.'

She works in the local squash club, she says. Keeps her amongst young people. She in her empty house can clearly feel the concrete creeping up the beach. Recalling Joseph Locke at the Club Tangerine on New Year's Eve: 'Same old Joseph, y'know — everybody was singin' with him and he was shouting, y'know. Y'see all those people have gone now and they're — y'see the Palace has gone, hasn't it? And Harold Mellor that was — er — head of the Palace. . . .' Her eyes stray listlessly round the room — 'he's died and — er — they've nearly all gone. Oh, and have you seen that terrible — um — nightmare — er — where the old Palatine was. That big concrete thing with those — Shocking — I don't know who the architect. . . .' She pauses. 'Well they're spoiling the pier really. I mean they're building all those Bingo places on the pier. At one time it was a lovely walk up the pier but now it's just covered in with all these. . . .'

Over coffee the talk tails off. Buddy Burgess will be out of his hangover and slapping on the after shave. I say my thanks and goodbyes. I feel terribly sorry for her and I feel rather embarrassed about the fact that it might show. She is proud enough to be offended.

4

William 'Buddy' Burgess in the saloon bar of the Farmer's
Arms is a different man from William 'Buddy' Burgess
trembling at the threshold while eight pints of lunch gallop
away into the past.

He is wearing his style along with his clothes, like most
people. He is also wearing his deaf-aid.

Frank Randle, he says, was a great comedian, a very very
funny man. Like most great comics he was concerned with
humour. Not wit, humour. Wit, says Burgess, is from the
head, humour from the heart. Burgess's personal style, hair
straight back, bright scarf, is the style of a journalist, a
small-town journalist who has lived his life in the midst of high
style and had some of it rub off. He speaks of theatre
personalities like John Capstack and Peter Webster, their
jaunty trilbies, their polka-dot dicky-bows, with a warm
appreciation for the bubbling naïve optimism which informed
them. He dives into his rich bag of stories with this chortling
affection for a way of life that was sharp, ebullient,
tongue-in-cheek and ruthlessly opportunist. Listening I'm
reminded that there's that about showbiz that is only a shade
away from the world of the race-track. Like gaming, music
hall was a back stairs up the social scale for the working class
and, being back stairs, the whole thing was something of a
caper, a bit of a lark, fortunes made and lost with a nudge and
a wink. 'They lived, you see,' says Burgess. 'They lived on a
scale that wouldn't be possible today.'

You couldn't control Randle, he says. Randle *knew*. Randle
always knew. The impromptu sessions with Gus Aubrey, Jack
Guy, Jimmy James, etc., he describes as though recounting
some kind of wild massacre. Throughout his talk he himself
has become a little incandescent. I oil the lamp with Bell's and
rescue Petal from the book about Picasso in which she has been
immersed. A quick hour in Yates's Wine Lodge that demands
a visit in Blackpool as the Mona Lisa demands a visit in Paris.
In the premises of the old Talbot Square Assembly Rooms, its
huge triangular chamber houses four or five separate bars, the
usual knots of people, and as much space as a railway station.
It is, in fact, very like a Victorian station waiting room. The
same long narrow floorboards. Notices everywhere. A cash

kiosk like a signal box and the station master/manager surveying all from his office window high in the wall over the main bar. We drink Manhattans at a bar where they serve draught champagne. I pop down to the Grill Bar to use the phone. Joseph Locke — no luck. A collection of twinkling old lads in loud check suits are enjoying their familiarity with one another at a twilit bar in the corner of the restaurant.

Closing time. A quick nosh. I pick up my photocopies from the *Gazette* office, then walk to the Winter Gardens complex to find Max Crabtree with whom I already have an appointment. I enter through the fairground. A man with a bit of Paisley silk double-knotted around his throat is hard at it, tuning up the Dodgem Cars. He directs me to Crabtree's office, a big, comfortable, shabby room where Crabtree eventually presents himself. A confident man, Crabtree treats me to his best front-of-house manner. He lists the shows in which Randle worked for 'us' — he recalls a few gags, a few anecdotes — Randle looks down the front of his shorts, gurgles, rolls his eye at the lady in the stalls, looks down again: 'A can see — A can see' — gurgles at the audience, keeps 'em waiting: 'A can see me feet!' — He is either cagy or genuinely innocent of anything discreditable and sends me on my rather unsteady way with faultless amicable politeness. Through the ebb-tide of the afternoon, where winking rubicund faces float amongst the tatters of play bills and the remote clink of glasses, I am beginning to realise that my cup of information is nearly full. A couple more people, a couple of outstanding facts, and, unless someone emerges with the key, the cornerstone to the multi-faceted structure that was Randle's personality, I have enough. As much as nicety of form permits.

Petal and I flee to Lancaster where the ambience is different and more congenial to Petal's superior taste. Outside Lancaster the car starts to make a noise like a steam hammer and shudders into the nearest garage where it stops.

We find a hotel like a student refectory in Lancaster. The cement society deserves its students and their boycott-the-sausage-rolls politics as it deserves the football savages. The next day a sleepy meandering bus takes us back across the Fylde to Blackpool.

5

John Lovelace, in whose letter handwriting darted like a stoat across the tiny notepaper, accepts our apologies for being late. Freda Lovelace, an eagerly hospitable woman with the noises and reactions of an excited child, seizes Petal by the forearm with both hands as though greeting a long-lost relative. Petal likes her. She likes anybody energetic and wonder-struck. She lacks my appetite for the seedy and the sardonic. John Lovelace, on the other hand, is objective, deliberate, with a certain urgency of purpose in wanting to talk to me. He is pleased to see the interview set up formally, with he and I sitting opposite one another in his sparsely furnished parlour. After mentioning a recent illness and implying that things haven't gone too well for him and Freda since, he launches into his account like a professional lecturer, occasionally silencing Freda's excited interlocutions with a brusque back-paddling of his hand. 'I worked for Jack Taylor back in 1934,' he says, settled well back in his chair. 'Joining him then at the Old Opera House and — er — he came with a show called *Thousand and One Marvels* — would be — '34 — and actually he was the first man to give Blackpool its season shows of twice nightly. Now people don't tell you all this. He tried it out with this *Thousand and One Marvels* and it was a success.'

Freda asks Petal if she wants more tea, dear, but is hushed abruptly with the extended hand.

'At the Opera House,' he goes on ''E 'ad, the following year, Billy Bennett.'

'Always a gentleman,' I interpose but Lovelace is in full spate.

'And it was a success and then, 'e 'ad a contract then with the Tower Company and the following year 'e put Albert Birdnip and the Four Franks — American act — and the following year Randle came along wi' George Formby. Now Formby and Randle didn't hit it — jealousy from the first week.'

The stories he tells are of incidents that gave him, Lovelace, and a good many others, reason to be apprehensive of Randle to say the least — wild bursts of temper, a generous amiable man who is suddenly invaded by the personality of a psychopath. He reveals a wellspring of manic sadism that overflowed the outward behaviour of a well-loved man with terrifying ease: 'A type of fella that if he didn't like you, you could get weavin' out of it and never cross 'is path again — Was testing you out whether you liked so-and-so in the show or not — He was one of them type of men and 'e was brewin' for somethin' up in 'is mind — The type of man who, I should say, probably 'ad a bit of female trouble with 'im. 'E was jealous of women. 'E was a disturbed fella. Don't forget, 'e was a boxer and a wrestler. Now whether 'is brain 'ad got disturbed in those years . . . got a knock, hit on the head . . . that I couldn't say because I wouldn't know. . . .'

At the same time he paints a clear picture of the way in which Northern promoters like Taylor and Brennan rocketed to wealth in the thirties — 'Then we went on tour and we played — er — the first date we played in London was — er —'

'What was the name of the show?' I ask.

'*Shout for Joy*,' he says emphatically. 'We played London date and I think we went to Holborn Empire. Now, then. A funny date, Holborn. We opened there — I'm sorry, not Holborn — I said Holborn. It was . . . Empire, just a minute. I'll 'ave to just. . . .' It comes to him. 'It was Holborn — I'm sorry, it was *Stratford* Empire. We opened there on the Monday night sixty minutes late because the production was such a large production — and we'd come from Blackpool not knowing that we — 'ow long it was going to take to fit up and the production was so heavy that it was impossible to open at 6.15 — twice nightly we 'ad to. It was fifty minutes late. We carried on and we went and played at all Moss Empire dates. We was on Moss Empires all of the winter from Glasgow down to the South back up to the Midlands and we played all the dates with Frank Randle. Not George Formby — Frank Randle.'

Lovelace's brother has been a theatre manager for many years and is still working in Southport. 'My brother worked for Brennan for a big number of years. 'E was 'is manager. My brother could 'a' come 'ere to the Queens many years ago. 'E didn't come. Johnny did it — was manager. 'E lived in Poulton I think. Oh yes, me brother worked for Brennan and 'e worked for Taylor. They was the two big men 'e ever worked for in the theatre. Never did tourin' like I did. I've bin tourin' for a number of people — Prince Littler, Jack Hylton, George

Elrick — took George Elrick out when he'd just come off the BBC — went out with a seven-piece band and that band was Lew Stone's — and I went out with a show called *Youth Must Have Its Swing* for Jack Hylton. And I started at the old Grande Theatre, Doncaster.'

These Blackpool show-people are like the survivors from a kind of explosion. For twenty years of their lives, the thirties and the forties, they were participants in a rocketing galaxy of wealth, laughs and spectacle. The conflagration has died down. Mecca and other emissaries of concrete have bought up the old firms, the old entertainment complexes, the Tower, the Winter Gardens, the Piers. Blackpool is looking a bit healthier just now (flexing its gaudy old limbs for the season that starts next week) than it did when I visited five years ago when Central Pier was closed and the Golden Mile looked like a set of abandoned allotment sheds in the cold westerly drizzle. None the less many of these people left moneyless, unprotected by the buoyant style that seems to carry some of their contemporaries, are stranded, bewildered and bored by the sheer emptiness of lives that were once so packed.

Lovelace is bitter about performers who forget. Youngsters he saw launched and who, comfortable now with Granada bit parts, don't recognise the old company chippy who was prepared to do anything from clowning to scene painting. This bitterness is somehow curiously linked with his anxiety to talk. He was part of the galaxy, deeply involved in something rather special and wonderful and he wants the world to know it. 'When you're on tour with a person,' he says, 'It's like your brother or sister. I mean to say, those dressing rooms are like your home for a week and when you're on tour — made quite a lot of theatre friends such as Frank Randle was one — er — They — Randolph Sutton was very — type of a good man to — um — under — quite a number of artists that I got on very very well with and they were more or less — I — They, they helped you. Frank Randle, for instance. Well, as I told you, he would go out of 'is way to 'elp. I've told yi — 'e 'ad a split personality and that's it. I left Frank Randle and I joined Jack Buchanan and Frank Randle wrote me a reference. Those curtains are comin' off, Freda.'

'Are they?' cried Freda as though this trivial mishap were some sort of miracle.

'Aye,' says Jack Lovelace, 'Thu're comin' undone. Thi've come off their pegs.'

6

The jalopy rots in Lancaster and Petal, snug on the Trans-Pennine Express, heads gratefully home to Yorkshire while I depart to Wigan and Skelmersdale. This is the last leg of the Lancashire tour. I had thought that the key was with Lovelace and I still think it must be with the ladies. No piece of information so far has clunked into place in a way which would identify it as the cornerpiece in the Chinese puzzle of Randle's fragmented character. The crock of gold at the end of the rainbow is, at the moment anyway, Queenie's address.

Wigan is small, friendly and busy. The large hotel by the station whose exterior promises a plush Victorian decor is, in fact, a rough, noisy boozer packed with grey comic faces. The beer is tepid and flat as Northern beer should be. The claque of the snooker balls punctuates the fuzzy throbbing of the juke box.

The Skelmersdale bus meanders aimlessly through knotty shopping streets, scabby patches of upland which mark the delineation between one village and another. Pools of greasy water stagnate beside semi-derelict mills and pit-heads. The luxurious in this region is shabbier than the roughest fare in the South and the people are busily content with the fact. They are bad at style and good at laughing. Their sensibility is a mutual irony about their ability to shape their lives without sensibility. Too sensible for sensibility, happy with function and fact, oblivious to ambiguity and mystery. They are inhabitants and functionaries of the Nation's arse, unceremonious, earthy, healthy, mutually content in the knowledge of their importance. They get on and off the bus speedily and noisily, recognising one another, talking across distances, unconcerned about eavesdroppers. There is an accord between their behaviour and the improvised functionalism of their little towns. Then, suddenly, the bus accelerates, climbs into a smooth arc of tarmac and we are out of it. The chatty industrious women and schoolkids, grizzled old colliers, who, one felt, had a firm and capable hand in the shaping of that scruffy, seething complex below the overpass, have nothing whatsoever to do with this bland system into which we move. The planners that nobody sees are the makers here and, with all the urbanity of a hospital matron or a school master, proceed to direct us to our different points of arrival. Here is your Town Centre says the notice and this is the way to get there. When, in fact, we do get there the town centre consists of a supermarket, a community-arts centre named after Nye Bevan, a pub and a car park. They all look like garages. Only the litter and aerosol graffiti indicate their human usage. Skelmersdale, doubtless a hard and bitter place to live in at the best of times, has been paved over.

Mrs Alma Thompson, Randle's niece, lives in a council house — red brick, front garden. She is just home from the factory and her son and daughter-in-law are just off to a caravan rally. The son describes the trap he's laid in the garage for vandals. Some scarved and booted Man. United supporter is likely to get a swift rock on the bonce. She despatches them, offers me a hot tea and a bed fort' night. When I decline both she serves sausage rolls 'fresh from t'butchers t'day', and tea, and she settles down to chat.

'From what I can gather 'e was born Arthur 'Ughes,' she begins with a Lancashire twang you could hang your cap on. It is a characteristic of the Hughes family to which she belongs that someone or other up and down the family tree inherits a comic creative flair. Hers is channelled into verses, some humorous, some reflective, philosophical, many in dialect, which she writes for the local paper and the works magazine. 'I don't know 'ow old 'e was when 'is mother married McEvoy, because A've only learned this whilst A've been askin' me mother things to tell you. Uh — ' Her glance searches out of the window where the spring sun is bright on new brick. A bay window is reflected perfectly in the right lens of her spectacles — ''e was livin' — er — A lady, this lady, in Wigan, luked after 'im, a Mrs 'Eath. 'E was with the 'Eath family while 'e was very young. They kept — '

'Until?' I interrupt.

''E kept in touch,' says Alma Thompson.

'Until he got a stepfather, probably,' I suggest.

'Well,' says Alma, 'while me auntie was workin', yes.'

She is, of course, letting me know that such temporary

adoptions were a neccessity in those days. She must keep the family free of accusations of dodged responsibility. 'They intended to get married,' she says, 'but 'e died y'see. A think 'e was in the army. A'm not sure.'

Mrs Thompson is informative about the family by and large, and especially keen for a clear class differentiation within the family. Rhoda, Frank's mother, was unlikely to have allowed him to work in a coal mine because her branch of the family, and indeed she herself, enjoyed the reflected gentility of having been in domestic service. She herself had been sent home from a pit-head job by a relative indignant to find her working there.

She remembers who attended the Randle funeral and provides me with a copy of the funeral invitation along with a number of press cuttings. She gives me Queenie's address, invites me round to meet her mother, and repeats her offer of an overnight bed. I decline the invitation to meet the old lady. I am, by now, swimming in information, much of it repetitive and some of it contradictory. My literary sense recoils from too rich a provision of ingredients. One or two facts I want and I am awfully afraid that when I get them I won't be able to use them.

The light sears down on the distant Pennines all the way back to Wigan. The taxi is reasonably cheap, one of the benefits of areas where concrete has impinged so thoroughly as to virtually decimate the local bus services.

On the station in Manchester I run into a member of Los Paranoyas comedy rock band. We sink canned beer as the train rockets through the shadows of the Calder Valley and talk about how bloody awful things are.

7

One day it will be my privilege not to conduct my professional life as a blade of purpose to be thrust through a dense fuzz of alcohol. But not today. There are always small celebrations along the way and, in any case, I share my subject's conviction that the whole of one's life is a celebration of one kind and another, and so deserves a toast.

Visiting Angela Flowers in her gallery is certainly always a celebration and it is from this pleasant occasion that I must extricate myself and make my devious way over the river and left, to where the river becomes broad and majestic and Greater London gets shuffled amongst the sedges and marshes of Kent. Two buses take me to a taxi and the taxi takes me through Greenwich to a place high on a hill with a green common and estates of semis looking down over the estuary. The spring air is clear and there is a pub on the corner of the appropriate street where I still have ten minutes or so in which to celebrate my arrival in the clean air.

Queenie's sister's house has steep steps up to the front door. Queenie, who has been painted through the mists of time as a kind of cross between Anna Neagle and the Queen Mother, is, in fact, a brisk cockney woman not exactly broken down with despondency at being widowed twice. She has smart white hair and a healthy sun tan. She doesn't look like the prisoner of Craig Royston and she doesn't look as though she harbours any secrets. Is the key going to prove to be a secret? Maybe it's been sticking out a mile all along.

Sister Wynn is in attendance, a burly extrovert woman who is a shade, just a shade, protective of her sister. She elbows her husband, a wise-cracking taxi driver retired, out of the interview fairly briskly and gets her powerful *obbligato* into the chat as she brings tea and sandwiches and cakes.

Thumbing through my bag for a notebook I come across Maisie Norris's letter. 'Remember her?'

'Oh yes,' says Queenie. 'Max and Maisie Norris. Now where's 'er brother, then? They'd a double act.'

I say that Max is maybe dead. 'Maxie?' she cried, as though having buried two husbands she still finds death ridiculously improbable. 'Well I'm blessed.' She reads on into the letter. 'She's right in everything she says there. They were a brother-and-sister act. Lovely act they 'ad. Well I'm bl —'

I ask the miner question for the last time. 'No — You asked in your letter didn't you? No. He never was, but when 'e was leaving school that was the talk, y'see. Everybody else was going down the mine. 'E-e-e-e wouldn't go down the — ' taking a cup of tea from Wynn — 'Thank you, luv.'

There is a complicity between these sisters. Two of a family of seven, brought up in a one-up one-down in New Cross. 'But it was a *happy* home,' says Wynn, 'a *happy* house. . . .' A number went into showbiz, including young Alfie who was a low comic — 'Dirty, y'know, dirty,' says Wynn.

I mention Arthur Delaney. Queenie is convinced that her husband was not the real father. Possibilities chase one another at breakneck speed through my mind as I grope hurriedly for the next question. Other lovers? White lies? But which white lies? By whom, to whom and why? It's difficult in these days to realise the awful stigma attached to illegitimacy only twenty years since as it's difficult to understand the horror of homosexuals and the scandalous impact of much of Randle's material. I mention, as tactfully as I can, that I'm not given to euphemistic writing — 'He was a rough old lad, your husband.'

'Oh he was,' she says, 'but you know, it's funny, because he was a most misunderstood man. He was very calm, very calm. He was lovable, he was gentle, but touch the wrong spot — Hoo-hoo-hoo. . . .'

Wynn joins in this crowing laugh. Part of their closeness is their echoing of one another's noises, laughs, tuttings, even words, a procedure which, despite the elaborate hospitality, indicates that at a deeper level I am an interloper and that these two are maintaining an amazing solidarity against any upsetting influence I might bring.

'But he was always justified. You know what I mean?'

'Justified,' says Wynn.

'He was always justified but he was a huh-huh, you know.'

'Huh-huh,'' says Wynn

Queenie recalls Mama Heath, tells me that Mama Heath nursed little Arthur through pneumonia when he was 6, recalls that George Formby was a childhood friend.

'He kinduv hated Formby, didn't he?' I ask. Her face bristles with indignation. 'No! No! I'll tell you the truth. 'E didn't, did 'e Wynn?'

'No, no . . .' says Wynn.

'Oh yes, we used to entertain — and they used to entertain us. He was very fond of Formby.'

I wonder if there are still corners of the land where men conduct their home life as a polite formality ten miles removed from life outside the domestic walls. I wonder if Beryl Formby was so estranged. I begin to see, in any case, that Queenie was

not merely estranged from the outside world in those boom
years. She was none too familiar with her old man. Did she feel
a prisoner in Craig Royston? 'Prisoner?' she says. 'Oh I did.
Definitely I did.'

'Definitely,' says Wynn.

She recalls Craig Royston with pride: 'D'you know, we 'ad a
beaut — Mind you, it would be old fashioned now — There
was a beautiful red mahogany suite — dining-room suite.
Beautiful, it was. They did say at the time that Anthony Eden
was the only one 'ad one like it. Well, 'e got it, this vicar' —
Craig Royston was sold for a vicarage — 'Beautiful Wilton
carpet 'e got and a lovely . . . er . . . Wilton carpet. . . . 'E
was a devil for giving things away.'

'He was good natured y'see,' says Wynn. 'True — if 'e liked
you you could 'ave anything.'

Queenie tells me that she toured with Randle for years after
she stopped performing herself. Finally she stopped touring,
she says, 'just to the latter end, and then I 'ad a companion
with me 'cos 'e was very jealous you know. Wouldn't let me
move.'

'Yes, I know,' I say, putting a teacup down soundlessly.

'D'you know that an' all?'' she cries.

'Yes,' I say.

'Oh Christ,' she says and shrieks with laughter.

Did she like living with Rhoda? 'Oh yes,' she says. 'We got on
very well together.'

''Very well,' says Wynn. The sisters are not too far removed
from the sisters Waters.

'Never a cross word all the thirty years. . . . A very nice little
person. Prim and proper, y'know. Not proper, no, she'd 'ave a
joke. Prim. Nice little person, wasn't she Wynn?'

'Nice,' says Wynn.

She recalls the Catholic wedding. Wynn recalls the
reception — 'The 'ole street was in it! Everybody in! Then we
'ad concert parties — There was — er — Alfie, and Queenie
was there — and we could 'ave singin' and dancin' and
neighbours complainin'. . . .'

'Talk abaht a lively 'ahse,' says Queenie, getting broad with
nostalgia.

'The neighbours outside said they loved it,' says Wynn. 'And

the neighbours opposite opened the windows and so they didn't
'ave a say down the end of the street. It was only one
person. . . .'

'Hm.' says Queenie.

'And — um — it was a really *'appy* place,' says Wynn, 'and
it was just a one-up-and-downer, y'know.'

Queenie rubs home the point of her husband's generosity
and how it was abused. She makes it clear that he ultimately
paid for the Hulme Hippodrome dressing room but Brennan
returned the hundred-pound cheque — 'coinage of the
realm. . . .' She recounts numerous incidents of kindness,
indeed she has little recollection of much else.

The buses back to the West End are few. A couple of days
later I am standing at the bar of the Faversham Hotel, a little
hideaway of red-brick Victorian Leeds isolated in the midst of
a concrete campus that is already dropping to bits. I am
matching Scotch for Scotch with Ken Smith, a tough and
highly companionable poet who looks like a cross between Dr
Crippen and Wild Bill Hickock.

'I should't be surprised —' I say.

'Inadvisable,' says Smith.

'Y'know, the possibility occurred to me — '

Queenie, Catholic and childless . . . Marjorie Taylor: 'or
anythin' . . . 'A gooz t' bed an' A gooz t' sleep'. . . .

' — Didn't. Ever. Not at all,' I say to Smith.

'It happened in those days,' says Smith. He looks into his
Scotch with a slight wince.

'A possibility,' I say, feeling as though a key has just dropped
through a hole in my trouser pocket.

PART VII

Love and Death and Arthur Twist

1

Theatre is a human root. Other arts are the province of the individual artist. Theatre is like architecture, religion, agriculture, marriage. It is rooted too deeply for comprehension, develops unperceived throughout the tribe until it is fully formed, a clear, finished complex face of the community's tacit values. Individuals may come to theatre and bend it, use it, suffer the delusion that the idiom offers them freedom. The theatre grows new fronds of its own volition as soon as any revolutionary limb-lopping begins. The individual in the theatre is overgrown, interpenetrated, sapped and succoured by primitive systems of energy as basic to the species as love and death. Innocent performers who thought to act out their own unique gifts become unconscious executants of primitive ritual duties.

Shakespeare, a man who knew this, was obsessed with kings because he knew that the coming into being of monarchs and the coming into being of theatre was, originally, the same human function. Randle, a man who did not know this, used theatre as a means to the privilege his personality demanded. He gave himself in innocence then, to ancient procedures fundamental to theatre. To theatre, to royal privilege and thence to sacrifice, to a subtly-wrought ritual death. No man is king in any real way unless he be also victim. The hero is a tough, big-hearted little chancer from Wigan. He has no way of understanding that his profession, if carried out with any real profundity, is the very home and expression of Nemesis.

The executioners gather round, as innocently as he awaits them.

2

Cinderella draws out better music from a monkey-skull with a barrel-organ mind. The hero takes a fistful of Christmas tenderness and sifts it like snowflakes into a fresh confrontation. The hero carries out secret solemnities over a pumpkin and a withy-broom. The witnesses are numbered in thousands. They file their benign dream-ranks down the aisles of the Hulme Hippodrome chanting hosannas, casting a confetti of torn paper hats.

There's the fairy on the wedding cake under her horseshoe. There's the fairy on the christmas tree with her bright frost. There's Mrs Risk, Rhoda and the Ice Queen isolate in the arctic palace on Lytham Road — all the polished places you could eat your disappointment off, all the glittering pinnacles as remote as the image of your lost mother in a star-kissed toyshop window. And then there's the secret bride beside you, close and tangible as Mama Heath, earthy as a loose-knit cardigan, bright as hoarded buttons of urchin mischief, sweet as allsorts, juicy as a jelly-baby.

A summer musk comes rippling off the Ribble hay. Bikes are knotted against a wall of bone-white stone. A Sunbeam with a smooth dip from saddle to tinkle-bell. A Hercules with leather and a hard bar. They grapple silently, afternoon hot on their bodywork, August rising from the musky groin of the Dale.

'What about first house, Frank?'

'Bugger first house. Life's too short for contracts.'

Time's running out like whiskey dregs. The waves of sickness rising like chloroform from the pit of every midnight. Dr Scollops's warning. Six years to go seven years ago. Rosebuds while ye may. No monkey up a stick can catch a fleeting blossom. Autumn petals only come to rest on noble brows. The belching monarch will shed his skin, stand forth with a new diction. *Hindle Wakes. Love on the Dole. A Lancashire Play.* Hamlet rises out of Caliban's dissolving pelt. The beast turns Prince of Denmark and lifts a glass of purifying flame to Dr Scollops and all the other twaddling quacks.

But the summer's running out and the gathered rosebuds are spilling along some lurching cobbled snicket. The Prince's proud tread skids into a winter of whiskey. Uneasy thespians dissolve a failed Act Two in a hasty Hallelujah Chorus. The only Cinderella left is Gus with a shirtful of cushion and his water cut off. The last summer starling takes a pert look at the haughty Stalin, at the Wigan Messiah and giggles her way away over the pit-heads.

Partake of the purifying elixir. Strain magic into the prancing flesh — daggers in the gut. Pour it into milk as pure as Queenie's breast. Swill it round a green sprig of asparagus. Swing with the careening footlights till you quiver up to a kingly stature. All stand. Coronation. Ladder to the heights of Heaven, carried up the rungs of Handel on the back of the St Christopher that hangs round your neck, and sack the Huddersfield pianist who quotes the MU rules and keeps his seat.

They'll know, the minions, the also-rans, the lame-brained underlings, that a cheated hero who can't catch rosebuds when the days get short can crack a pistol, whang fast slugs around the sterile Mancunian film-set, twanging ricochets off camera rings. The hero, dragged back into his ape-skin by a tongue that only dances in the sewer, can relax in a wrecked dressing room, shattering miniatures with pistol bullets, peppering glass shards into cold cream, propelling Jimmy Clitheroe down the backstage labyrinth yelping like a stung mongrel. A lawsuit for Locke and an axe in a paper bag for Taylor. Strut through the rehearsal armed to the teeth. One word from thee Jack Taylor and I'll splatter thi skull to damson jam. Nobody directs the world's greatest actor, nobody.

An altar is erected where the baby bottles burst in sharp stars. Knocking upstarts shouting urgencies through locked doors can be told: 'Fuck off! Can't you tell I'm praying?'

Let Cinders and elusive rosepetals float away in the arms of Peter Hindley who fouled *Namouna*'s salt air with his lecheries, of Bobby Beaumont, the milk-sop brother-in-law of George Black. The Watch Committees may berate the hero's grovelling tongue and the antics of tormented flesh, but he'll tell the cub reporter from the *Wolverhampton Express and Star* that the world is starved for want of prayer. He'll tell the crowing Oldham audience that claps for monkeys how the greatest man of all was stable-born. The rosebuds flutter into doctors' promises. The spike spurts streptomycin into flesh gone carrion for sustenance of others and the Ice Queen looms again into prominence, the aurora borealis of the Mother Church housing her immaculacy in visible music.

The only true face is the face of Queenie. The only true word is the word of the Lord. Executioners are St Anthony's menagerie. Masks, great Hallowe'en heads. Somewhere in the city of Cardiff Cinderella is drowning in milksops. The gargoyles gather twittering round the backstage tea-urn. The owls with scaly backs snicker over the dressing-room whiskey. They tell clipped jokes about what happened to the summer, chant dirty limericks about traffic jams in Cinderella's bed. The hero stands remote as a wedding-cake groom at the bar of the Park Hotel. The stagehand sent to fetch him is a little man, an old and unassuming friend. The hero acquiesces, does his thirty minute turn. Then the black-hood rage comes down in blood and bile behind his eyes. The bullet-startled Clitheroe hits gloss-painted backstage bricks like a bean bag. The manageress finds her body-bolsters of mammary marsh-mallow hung by the bra-straps and dress rags from dressing-room hooks. Lecherous voices sing finger-sniffing songs along the phone wires of the Park Hotel. The telephonist breaks into dithers. The nerve-ends of Babylon hang cut worms from the switchboard sockets. Every theatrical lodging-house in Cardiff, every greasepaint B & B, will know the brickbats of the Lord smash thunderbolts into their cells of snide fornication.

Rain lashes a whiskey-smudged windscreen. Harlequin and Columbine are thistledown in the headlights. Sooty eyes and holly-berry lips behind the weather's diagonal needles, and a wrenched wheel makes the bonnet into a swift missile. They leap into obscurity and the lamp-crome's clear of love-blood. Get a grip McEvoy. Need a drink.

Dragon heads amass. Colleagues are lethal dolls with their Tussaud paint and their ghost-train cackles. Oblivious of the sermon sewn into the hero's every act they must be shown supernatural power in the wielding of dressing-room door lead, in rubber-band play with a chest-expander. They must be summoned onstage to be whipped into physical training. The Hallelujah Chorus rings through the halls of the Lord. They must be corrected.

Coynes in his Boy Scout uniform with the whistle on his lanyard follows the bikini girl on with a 'Hello, Grandpa'.

Sotto voce: 'Get off! Get off the fucking stage!'

Aloud: 'Eeh now young man, is your whistle dangling?'

Coynes, *sotto voce*: 'I came on as rehearsed, Mr Randle.'

Aloud: 'Yes, it is Grandpa.'

Randle, *sotto voce*: stick raised over the table of the Dog and Duck: 'Get off the fucking stage!'

Coynes, *sotto voce*: 'No.'

Bring the stick down within a blade's breadth of Coynes's fingers. Aloud: 'Dangling eh! Your very fortunate. . . .'

In the dressing room, the sanctum, the holy place whence the tongues of spirits speak through a mouth imprisoned by the sorry restrictions of the flesh — 'Christ, listen to him. He's off again. . . .'

'Coynes!'

'Yes, Mr Randle.'

'Coynes, you will never, never reach a true level of artistry unless you call upon the power of the Father.'

'No, Mr Randle.'

'You will never, Coynes — ' — Pour a stiff one — fill the tumbler — 'never surmount the wretched imperfections of your performance until you submit to the disciplines of prayer.'

'No, Mr Randle.' See his terror of the Kingdom registered in the dithering of his baggy shorts.

'Coynes, you are a *cunt*!'

'Yes, Mr Randle.'

'But I like you. Drink that.'

Like a bloody cripple in the second half. No stamina. Repel the ghouls. Dissolve them in whiskey, drown them in sad rain. 'I'm a Good Boy Now' at the Norwich Hippodrome and a bouquet of lost roses at the Theatre Royal. No callboy breathless at the stage door shaking the rain out of his cap, bearing a rose petal in his grubby fist. No bouquet of summer waiting in the wings.

'Coynes,' growled over a last glass.

'Yes, what is it Frank?'

'She'll be back.'

'Yes Frank. She'll be back.'

3

Unknown Newspaper. Early 1954

TWO SHOWS GO ON ONE STAGE

There were more people on the stage of the Empire Theatre, Oldham, for the finale of the second house show last night than there were in the audience.

For it was 11 o'clock and there had been two shows in one on the stage. An alleged booking mix-up was blamed.

Originally there was to have been a variety bill, headed by Ken Frith, pianist in the BBC's 'Al Read Show.'

Then on Saturday Frank Randle and his new company arrived. Randle tried to merge the two shows. On Monday night it over-ran an hour.

RALLY ROUND

RANDLE said yesterday, 'When I found there was a mix-up I took responsibility for both shows. I asked everybody to rally round. Shortened acts had to be rushed on and off.'

MR J. SULLIVAN, the theatre's manager, said: 'Randle's show was booked by our agents when they found he had a free date this week.'

KEN FRITH said: 'At the theatre nothing seemed organised. I've never seen anything like it.'

Last night the trimmed shows still had two xylophone acts and two sets of chorus girls. Ken Frith's act did not appear at the second house.

Unknown Newspaper. January 1954

They Call Themselves The Good Companions. Sonny Roy is at the piano.

CURTAIN UP ON SHOW WITHOUT A BOSS

Twenty former members of Frank Randle's pantomime Cinderella, who broke with their comedian employer after matinee payment disputes, are back in show business tonight — as the Good Companions of 1954. They opened at the Hippodrome, Accrington, claiming to be the only show without a boss, and the nearest parallel to J. B. Priestley's Good Companions ever reached on the British halls.

'Happiness and peace of mind are the main things needed to make a good show,' said 31 year old Sonny Roy, the elected manager, when the company reached Accrington yesterday.

They went into the theatre as lions from last week's circus left the stage. And Mr Ross Jones, the theatre manager, was waiting with the good news that their agent had booked them for a seven week tour.

They were on stage rehearsing almost immediately — without orders.

NO NEED FOR STARS

'You see the harder we work, the better it is for us,' said Ernie Dale, the baritone who worked 14 years for Frank Randle.

'We split the profits and take an equal share,' explained Sonny Roy, who turned down a £35-a-week contract in Ireland to stay with the company.

'It is lovely,' said Kay Sothern, who was Randle's principal boy.

'We all work together,' said the Peters Brothers, Kevin and Charles in one breath.

'And,' added comedian Roy, 'just as long as we stay together we can make a living. We are all experienced performers. We can give a show with talent and without star names. We have nothing to bump up costs.'

Already they plan to put the whole cast into pantomime next winter — in the same parts they played in Randle's Cinderella.

Unknown Newspaper. January 1954

NOW RANDLE SENDS CAST A LETTER
by Michael Walsh

Frank Randle has sent a solicitor's letter to Bernard Woolley, the theatrical agent who plans to put on the sacked members of Randle's company at Accrington Hippodrome on January 25.

The letter threatens action to protect Mr Randle's rights if any of them 'uses part or whole material from his show or colourable material thereof. . . .'

The sackings followed disputes about payment for matinees during the run of 'Cinderella' at the Empire Theatre, Middlesbrough.

NEW SHOW

The actors demanded full pay and Randle retaliated by making them perform to an empty house.

Said Mr Woolley: 'These boys and girls must be given a chance to earn a living. Some of them had served Randle loyally for nearly 20 years.'

Most of the company will stay on in Middlesborough this week rehearsing their new show.

They will work — like Priestley's 'Good Companions' — on an equal shares for all basis.

Unknown Newspaper. February 1954

FRANK RANDLE: I ACCEPT YOUR CHALLENGE

Mr Ross Jones, manager of the Hippodrome, Accrington, made theatre history in the early hours of today when he persuaded comedian Frank Randle to accept a challenge to follow his former cast at the Hippodrome next week.

This is the inside story of how it happened — I was there.

Behind the scenes of the Hippodrome last night when 'The Unemployed Scandals' — 18 ex-members of Frank Randle's Scandals who broke with Randle after a matinee payment dispute 12 days ago — opened their own 'Good Companions' Show. Mr Jones told me: 'I am going to

Blackpool to sign Frank Randle for next week. Will you come?'

Thirty minutes later he promised his first house audience: 'I will get you Randle next.'

Another 30 minutes and we were speeding towards Blackpool through snow in a 48-minute dash to the Queen's Theatre, where Frank Randle was opening his 'New Scandals.'

'If he throws me out you will still get a story,' said Mr Jones.

At the Queen's Theatre Mr Jones told Mr Randle's manager, 'I will pay him up to £750 to come to Accrington.'

'He will see you,' said the manager.

At eleven o'clock the curtain went down and Mr Jones and Frank Randle began to negotiate.

Soon after midnight the deal was clinched, and the two announced their agreement, arms round each other's shoulders.

Burly energetic Mr Jones, perspiring and chain-smoking, told me: 'I promised Accrington Frank Randle and I have got him.'

Mr Randle, immaculate, grinning wide, and slapping Mr Jones on the back, said: 'Mr Jones has talked me into it. I go to Accrington bearing no grudge against my former company. I hope they do very well.'

Later — around 2 a.m. — Randle the philosopher dictated a letter to the Good Companions.

He told me: 'I think this will be a great fillip to show business and a grand tonic to the boys and girls in Accrington.

'So long as there is no venom in it, it is all right.'

He gave me permission to use that letter. Here it is:

'Dear Lads and Lassies,

At this stage of the proceedings I do in all sincerity wish you good fortune. I admire your guts as always, and I still retain a liking for you as I have always had. And now that you have all flown from the edge of the nest I do trust that the storms you may weather may not be too inclement.

'If there is anything I can do, please let me because, in the words of a mental giant, in my humble opinion, "I only pass once this way." On this occasion I will pass after you. The

first shall be the last and the last shall be the first. I know
Accrington will not let you down.

'Accrington has never let me down, therefore, naturally,
it is beyond the realms of possibility that it should happen in
your case.

'Forgive Father-Mother Carey for following in the wake
of his-her chickens. I do hope that you have left me enough
scratching ground. Naturally the mother allows the chickens
to have the first pickings of the food and will be content with
what is left, which, in my humble opinion, will more than
suffice for the nonce.

'Good luck to you all and may you not have to plough the
hard furrow that your mentor has had to in the past.
Perhaps one day I may have the pleasure of working for you.
        'Yours most sincerely,
            Frank Randle.'

Past 3 a.m. today Mr Jones and I reached Accrington
again. At Accrington there was no snow, and Mr Jones had
smoked all his cigarettes but he had that remarkable
contract his energy and determination won him. He had
carried off the double-coup — Frank Randle's ex-company
one week, and Frank Randle with his new company to
follow.

It was the latest chapter in Mr Jones' fight to save a
theatre that has three times been threatened with closure in
the last 12 months.

TEETHING TROUBLES
Competition from the town's first floodlit football match cut
the first hour attendance at the Hippodrome to £18 last
night but the show was really on and the Good Companions
of 1954 are off the dole.

Everyone in the cast worked with spirit of adventure.
They had their troubles. They were short of tambourines. A
last minute dash to the Salvation Army at Blackburn Citadel
brought help from Senior Captain Rich who rang a music
shop which produced 18.

Unknown Newspaper. February 1954

FRANK RANDLE HUSTLE WINS
Even the Americans haven't anything on Frank Randle
when it comes to hustle.

Last night he presented himself and a huge supporting
cast at the Queen's Theatre, Blackpool.

Seventy-two hours earlier there had been only himself and
400 written applications in answer to his advertisements in
stage journals.

During that 72 hours telephone calls went out all over the
country. The result — a production which, with a few deft
touches, will become a highly entertaining show.

His achievement is the more remarkable because only 24
hours before the show was due to open he discovered that his
truckload of scenery had disappeared from a Blackpool
siding. Improvisation with available backcloths and curtains
was necessary last night. The show comprises a number of
variety acts blended into a non-stop entertainment with
Randle in several of his well-known character roles,
including 'The Old Hiker.'

Daily Express. 28 December 1954

GIRLS CALL POLICE TO PANTO COMIC
The princess, 22-year old Joy Zandra, was in tears. The
chorus girls walked off the stage. The cast phoned the
police.

It happened during a rehearsal of Aladdin at the Theatre
Royal, Oldham.

And after it comedian Frank Randle was sacked from his
job as Twanky the principal comic.

Said theatre manager James Bowers last night: 'I have
sent him a letter saying his contract has been broken by his
behaviour and asking him to collect his things.'

What happened to cause Twanky's hurried exit from the
panto? Explained Mr Bowers: 'Last Wednesday he did not
turn up for rehearsal. On Friday he arrived half an hour
late.'

NOT FIT

'He sat in the stalls and swore. He then went to the dressing room and I gave the part to Gus Aubrey, the Dame.'

Panto policeman Ray Lamar said: 'If he had come back the show would have walked out.'

And while the show went on without him last night Frank Randle said: 'I am going to sue them. I have a doctor's certificate to say that on Friday I was suffering from anxiety neurosis and exhaustion and, in the doctor's opinion, I was not fit to work.

'I did not raise my voice, I did not use bad language. I said "Let's get on with the job."'

4

The shades come to the hotel room as visitors. The emissaries, executioners, gather round. He knows an executioner when he sees one. Took the bombshell Dors to see Albert Pierpoint (a friend, of course, we men of *consequence*. . .) — don't know if she got the message. Those who have ears to hear. . . . Wages of sin. . . . They gather round. The man who bustles up, as clear of visage as an April day: 'My wife would like to meet you, Mr Randle,' and there she is with blind eyes of snot-coloured granite, a shade as sure and certain as any standing by the hotel wardrobe. People should know better.

The phone goes. 'Mr Coynes to see you, Mr Randle.' God's light. God's little fishes. God's truth. Where did my brain go? Down in Wigan fish market stretched on a slab. With prayer, a certain clarity — on yes, a fine morning disporting itself across the pastoral swales of Huddersfield.

A little pick-me-up, Ronné, and we'll be off. A long way to Reading. Certainly, certainly. It is. A swift medicinal and we'll be on our way. Breakfast? Why not? Baghum, young feller, an excellent idea. . . .

The hotel restaurant raises its columns, its embossed ceiling over the two little clowns like a cathedral over the heads of penitents. A certain poison in the air? Waiter! A window open, if you please. But sir, the other guests. . . . Are you aware my man, that you are addressing the greatest comic actor the world has produced? A window? Yes, Mr Randle. Certainly, sir.

What is this on my plate? Can you distinguish the nature of the refreshment, Ronné? It's dark as the bloody tomb in here Ronald, and it's getting darker. Could we, by any small chance, have a real light bulb in the light, waiter? One that works? What? Well bloody well find one!

Now then, Ronné. A stout breakfast. A leisurely journey. Perhaps a bite to eat on the way, but just before we embark — Waiter, is the bar open? Sorry, Mr Randle, the bar isn't open till twelve. Well then, you impertinent ignoramus, open the fucking thing. Are you aware that you are speaking to the greatest. . . . Do you think, do you imagine that I, an artist, give a fuck for your bloody licensing laws? A want a drink. My money is good. Are you aware. . . .

The star appears in Reading a day late. He turns in a tolerable performance. Still do it. Not finished yet, by Christ and St Christopher. What if the taxman collects his miserable fifty-six thousand? What if Joe, the Irish get, has the whole of the Imerald Oile to hide in? Sell Craig Royston, move Queenie and the Risk woman to a bungalow on Bispham Road. What if Queenie, God reward her, sells her jewellery. Not done, not done by a long bloody chalk.

Northampton. 'Good to see yer, Frank,' the man shouts as the comedian clumps on. It's the tenor of the voice, you see. A man of insight hears voices perpetually. Something above the roar of the audience, something after the roar has died, interrupting and diverting a perilous opening line.

'You sir,' the star says, fixing his fan with a turkey's eye, 'are a cunt. Get out of the theatre.' The manager will be summoned. The man will be expelled from the theatre before a line of the act is delivered. And the audience, bewildered, will have their mollification. The star's personality fills the theatre like light. A mistake perhaps, but a great man is a man who turns his mistakes to triumphs by reorganising the world about them. Rhetoric, the gift of tongues; the audience is satisfied. Anthony has turned the mob against Brutus. ' . . . And now ladies and gentlemen, let us continue.'

Fill in for Formby? *King Fun* hasn't been forgotten, even if people are forgetting who King Fun really is. Empty house at Stretford. Takings falling. The tide of twaddle, strippers, and real filth, comics who lean on evil gags, not vulgar, evil. I was never a *dirty* comedian. Fill in for Formby in a show with Jimmy James? The star hasn't forgotten the night in the Clifton when James had the bloody nerve to offer him that song he'd originally written for Hutch, 'I Wish There Was No Moon.' — A hint about a man's mental condition? A hint to drive a man of sensitivity straight out of the bar. The star has exorcised his madness in his new sketch. The men in white coats come on. 'Here you are then. You've left your windmill behind. We've brought you your little windmill.' 'That's not my windmill. Mine goez round t'other way.' There are those who will never distinguish between the gifts of the Lord and the madness of the moon. Jimmy James should know better. The hiker is supposed to clump down the aisle to cover for Formby and the hiker will not. The hiker will clump onstage in a charity show at Fleetwood because the star knows that the little people are the big people, big enough to know how small and how big a big man is. 'The biggest man who ever lived was born in a stable.'

No, there's no defeat. Even if he couldn't finish the week at Reading, even after the tax has been paid, Craig Royston sold for a vicarage, Queenie's jewellery sold. Go back to your root. Burn the Scandals, scenery, props, costumes, the bloody lot, in a gigantic bonfire at Rochdale. Go back to the Accrington Hippodrome, where the people were unsatisfied with the sacked Scandals, knew who their king was, sent their emissary through the blizzard, Accrington Hippodrome where Arthur Twist first carried on the Indian Clubs for the Roy Brothers while Eva Delaney stood in the wings. Turn the old Hippodrome into a new kind of theatre — good stuff, quality music.

And even after that flops and the hero himself flops fallen in a pile of rags on the Opera House stage exactly as he fell in a ragpile from his own car outside the Farmer's, after the last zigzag flight from Morecambe, the driving ban, the crippling fine, the magistrate's instructions that whiskey was insufficient cure for TB, that the course of therapy must be followed to the full, even after the humiliation of his own tears in court when he learned that Queenie would have to be told, even after all that, there's something left.

The folk in the hospital aren't the kind to steal your dreams and sell 'em behind your back.

'You learn the meaning of a few words said with hands clasped, and said in real sincerity. You learn to appreciate others who are used to being pleased with the most humble little benefits, to have tolerance and humility, perhaps for the first time in your life. People come to see you and bring you little things calculated to please you, without any idea of something in return except your smile of thanks.'

There's to be a show with real people in it, cast by, and of, the little people who never forget you and never let you down. Call it *King Cotton*. Manager Jim Munro and the Star are working on a new movie to be called *Wigan Peer*, like that, with a double 'e'. That should put the record straight. No, there's no defeat. Whiskey is the cleanser, whiskey and milk and the hand of God which touches more closely and more comfortably when finally, at long last, the hero makes it into Queenie's church.

Arthur McEvoy died on the morning of July 7th, 1957, of gastro-enteritis, and was buried in Carlton Cemetery. The family gathered round from different smoky corners of Lancashire. Stan Laurel was among the many great entertainers who communicated their grief.

Queenie found a verse in his wallet and had it cut on to his gravestone.

'I got nothing that I asked for
But everything I had hoped for.
Despite myself my prayers were answered.
I was among all men richly blessed.'

On waking on the morning of his death, a few minutes before he made his last walk down the hall of the bungalow, Frank Randle said: 'I'm worried about Gus. I don't think he's happy.'

And after that he said nothing.

Finale:

My Little Pal

Dear Sir,
    Replying to your letter of 28.4.77 I will do my best to answer as many of your requests as possible, but you will have to excuse my writing as I have been in hospital for five weeks having an operation on both eyes. Sorry to say I have lost the sight of the left eye but can see with the right thank God.
    You ask of the home Arthur was brought up in, Tom my late husband told me he remembers the day Arthur Hughes came to live with Mrs Heath he was brought there by a woman and both Tom and I met her at Arthur's home in Blackpool the day before he was buried at Carlton Cemetery and she recognised Tom when she met him there, also a member of the Heaths family was there too, but as she was older than Tom and Arthur the chances are she will have past on by now, and I do not know her name or where she lived. Tom said they were nice people and always kind You ask of his home it was just a little cottage in the same row as Tom's home.
    This was called New Square and off Standish Gate, Wigan Lane, they were built at the back of shops which played a big part in the enjoyment of the two little boys my husband had been a sick man for 13½ yrs before he died but he loved to tell me all the things they used to do when they played together and enjoyed each others company. They were both used to

better times and this is why they were different to the other
boys, Tom didn't know how he got to know the broad folk as
quoted in your letter it must have been later in his teens, after
Tom had left New Square, Arthur came to see Tom on his
18th. Birthday to tell him he was going to Blackpool to live
with his Mother and she had married Mr. McEvoy and he
understood Mr McEvoy kept a public house in B.pool.

Tom never saw Arthur again until he came to do a show at
Wigan Hip he had seen films of Frank Randall but he wouldn't
believe it was Arthur although he recognised the sand dance
they used to do, and this starts No 1 story.

1. There was a hat shop and gown shop at the back of their
homes and they used to dress up in ribbons and feathers and
hats and pieces left for the dust man to take away and this is
where the sand dance was first made up, Tom said they used to
have lots of fun just the two of them together.

2. This is another true story and one which gave them
something to look forward to.
Another shop was run by a very kind woman called Mrs
Dix's or Dicks I don't know how it was spelt, but every night
Tom and Arthur used to wait until the shop was empty and
they would go and sit at a round marble-topped table which
had iron legs and she would serve them with a plate of tripe
bits and cow heel salt pepper and vinegar, she never asked for
money in fact they had none, but it was taken for granted, she
must have been fond of them, and also she must have been a
very kind person and this was the high light of their day.

3. One of the places near by was a fruit warehouse and they
used to help the people bring home the fruit left over from
there market stalls and the owners used to tell them to fill their
pockets with oranges and they used to help themselves to the
grape barrels. this was another thing taken for granted.

4. There was also a toy shop near which had a cracked window
with a tiny little hole in the corner, Tom said they used to
spend hrs with a piece of wire trying to get a toy to the hole,
they knew they could never get one out but they had a good
imagination but they never did any damage the man used to

see them but said nothing to them (I remember *this* shop and I did not live in Wigan I lived in the country, but it was well known.)

5. Tom used to be fond of a tale he told of a Sunday School outing but they were not members and they wanted to go, it seemed a man put a blue stamp on the backs of the boys hands so Tom and Arthur got two boys to press their hands on the back of theirs whilst the ink was wet and off they went on a boat from Wigan Pier Wallgate no doubt you will have heard of Wigan Pier, the trip was to Gathurst 4 miles on the canal and they were given a bag of food and sweets and they sang.
    (Let the Blessed Sun Shine in)

Tom said they felt like Kings and had a good day and was never found out I think this was lovely Tom as told me of this many times. My eye is getting very tired so I will have to leave off until tomorrow.

Tom went to Wigan Hip he said he would find out if Frank Randal was Arthur Hughes or not. Arthur came out of the stage side door and he put his arms round Tom and said 'Tommy Hall my little pal' so they went to celebrate at the Shakespear a pub long taken down.

Frank asked Tom to take me and our daughter to see him that night after and we went in the wings and he told me the last story himself. so here goes; They wanted to go to Appley Bridge the village Tom was born in, but they had no money, so Tom sold a pen knife he had been given for his birthday and the fare was 2½d each return and they had one penny left, he told me they found a hens nest under a tree and they sucked a egg and enjoyed it Tom had forgotten this until Arthur told it to me. it seemed strange I should hear the last tale from Arthur himself and he said he was sorry I had met him dressed up as Grandad and Tom felt sorry he had gone so broad but he was happy to see him he had tears in his eyes as he told me of Tom selling the knife for 6d. that shows he never forgot after all all those years and it seems so strange we were at Blacpool on holiday when he died and we saw him for the last time.

Queenie his wife said it was his own show people that had let him down, all I know I could tell he was a very sick man the time I saw him at Wigan Hip. Arthur would have been a far happier man if he had lived like we did not a lot of money but a lot of love and understanding. Tom and I had 46 years of happiness he was 73 when he passed away and still as happy as a sandboy. I miss him very much. I am now 70 yrs I hope I have been able to help you with all this I do wish you had let me know the reason for wanting this information you know curiosity killed the cat.

I often wished I had tried to write a book of my Tom's life there are lots more he told me but it is too late now and my eyes are not good at all.

Oh one other thing I forgot. I don't know for sure but I think Arthur went to work in a shop and he was 18 when he went to live at Blackpool after that they lost contact until the Wigan Hip and the little Square where they lived as been taken down this last four year, and is now a car park.

Tom's father was a manager of a brick works but he died when Tom was only 3 yrs old and that was how Tom got to New Square. his mother went to Wigan when her money ran out to find work.

Yours sincerely
Florence Hall.

PS Tom and I came back to Appley Bridge as soon as we could and have lived here 46 years and Tom's remains are in the Village Garden of Rememberance, St Annes, Skevington.